THE MAKEUP OF ME
My Unmasked Truth

Courtney Hawkins

Published by Broken Branches Inc.

Book Design: Calvin Finklea WWW.CALVINFINKLEA.COM

All Scripture taken from the New King James Version of the Bible unless otherwise noted.

ISBN: **978-0692567807**

We Wear the Mask

WE wear the mask that grins and lies,
It hides our cheeks and shades our eyes, —
This debt we pay to human guile;
With torn and bleeding hearts we smile,
And mouth with myriad subtleties.

Why should the world be over-wise,
In counting all our tears and sighs?
Nay let them only see us,
While we wear the mask.

We smile, but, O great Christ, our cries
To thee from tortured souls arise.
We sing, but oh the clay is vile
Beneath our feet, and long the mile;
But let the world dream otherwise,
We wear the mask!

- Paul Laurence Dunbar

THE MAKEUP OF ME
My Unmasked Truth

Foreword

"If I go up to heaven, you are there; if I go down to the grave, you are there…"
Ps. 139:8 (A Psalm of David).

A causal reading of the psalms of King David will give you a glimpse into the colorful, and yet, complex life of the one God calls "A man after my own heart." What we know about David regarding what he felt and thought during some of the most difficult times of his personal life we know simply because he told us. David shared his pain and his moments of praise in prose and psalms for his generation. Through preservation of Holy Scripture we too gain insight into the life of David.

Just about every house I've ever seen has more than one window. The windows are generally placed in strategic places of the home to provide natural light and wonderful views to the outside world. Those same windows, however, also provide a view into the inside of the home. Each window provides a different sight. Anyone who has the ability to look in can not only see the inside of the home, but one could get a sense of the lives of those who live there.

Like David, Courtney Hawkins has chosen to share some of her most intimate trials, thoughts and triumphs. Courtney not only brings you to the window of her life, but in some cases she brings you in the room! I was blessed, to be in one of the rooms. I watched God, as in the case of David, "be there" for her as He has for so many down through the ages.

Courtney does a remarkable job of marrying pain, principle and purpose in this book. The "make up" of Courtney Hawkins is that of one, who through sheer strength of will, finds a way to live through it all! From brokenness to blessedness, Courtney's testimony is nothing short of a miracle. She has reached a place in her own healing process to be a blessing to someone else. Reading this book will allow you to see your own "makeup", and learn how to unmask your own truths. I'm very proud of her efforts in this first book. This book is an example of how to "provide answers for mankind's problems that will lead to abundant living." Congratulations "C$" you did it!

Pastor Darrell L. Fairer
Faith Bible Tabernacle, Buffalo, NY

THE MAKEUP OF ME
My Unmasked Truth

INTRODUCTION

The Makeup of Me: My Unmasked Truth tells the story of some of my life experiences: same-sex molestation at a young age and causing an accident that tragically claimed another's life. The experiences I share here expose the parts of me that were filled with self-hatred, guilt, shame, inadequacy, incompetence, depression, anxiety and severe thoughts about suicide. However, my story does not end there.

Ultimately, I became determined to break free of generational bondage so that I could live a life of abundance; therefore I surrendered my fears and accepted the transformational power of forgiveness, grace and mercy for my life that is legally bestowed to me as a child of God. Now I continually practice self-love while embracing my natural beauty, flaws and all.

Historical Context

The word *cosmetae* was first used to describe female Roman slaves whose function was to beautify their wealthy mistresses with *cultus* the Latin word encompassing makeup, perfume, and jewelry. Cosmetics have been used for as long as there have been people around to use them. Because the Romans preferred fair white skin, most people had to rely on face painting to lighten their complexions. Hence, the dawn of covering up one's real identity to appear to be something one is not.

Makeup has been used for countless generations as a powerful apparatus of transformation that virtually anyone can use. Not only women, but men also have adorned themselves with it for years. Although the practice was frowned upon by society and they were considered immoral, many men also used whitening cosmetics to alter their skin tone.

A primary motive for using makeup is to make one more attractive by masking imperfections and flaws. Makeup users thought that accentuating those imperfect attributes would make them more visually alluring not only to themselves but also to modern society. Today, some apply makeup to achieve a natural look. The goal is to give the illusion that they are wearing nothing at all.

However, in the same way, some apply makeup in the natural to cover physical blemishes and scars, these same individuals display tendencies to implement it to their imperfections and sins in the spiritual.

Flaws and imperfections can be an embarrassment to many people, not only what we judge to be flaws in our physical appearance but in our self-concept, low self-esteem being just one example of this. Because many of us lack the courage and confidence needed to accept and embrace our flaws we misrepresent ourselves by covering them with masks. Have you ever experienced wearing makeup and believing that you had on the bare minimum, thinking that no one will notice? Then someone asks the embarrassing question, "Are you wearing makeup?" It's at that moment you realize that what you thought was concealed is more noticeable to others than you think.

This book gives you an eye into my diary of healing. It is not solely intended for the religious. However, rest assured that my religious beliefs will be conveyed with thoughtfulness and an understanding that all may not share in my beliefs. It is my desire that my religious beliefs and experiences don't obstruct you from allowing yourself to benefit from the revelations I came to and sought to share with you here.

I have not set out to provide you with a step-by-step, how-to instruction manual on how to unmask your truth. On the contrary, I will assist you in uncovering vital insights. If you choose to heed them, these ideas will guide you into embracing your truth(s).

Just as we are all individuals with a unique set of DNA, the healing process for each is as unique. This book will provide you with a broad spectrum of information. The hope is that you will discover within its pages the written keys that will unlock your truth that can support you in setting yourself free.

Understand that I am not offering legal or medical advice with this book. I am only sharing my experiences and sharing some of the steps I have taken to heal. I am not a psychologist, physician, attorney or medical professional. If you are or believe that you may be, suffering from symptoms of any of the things I have spoken about above, immediately seek out the help of a professional.

THE MAKEUP OF ME

CONTENTS

Chapter 1 ………………………………………..…11
IDENTITY THEFT

Chapter 2………………………….......................23
COURT'S CASE

Chapter 3…………………………………………..30
BLACK DOES CRACK

Chapter 4………………………………………......42
MASTER OF DISGUISE

Chapter 5……………………………………………..50
ADDICTED TO LOVE

Chapter 6………………………………………......61
TEACH ME HOW TO LOVE

Chapter 7………………………………………......80
BEAUTY AND THE BEAST

Chapter 8…………………………….......................89
BEAUTY FOR ASHES

Chapter 9………………………………………......100
MY FOUNDATION

Chapter 10………………………………………......110
EMBRACELET

1

IDENTITY THEFT

DNA

As we seek wisdom for the future, it's important to have an understanding of our past. We have heard the adage "History repeats itself" and bear witness to the fact that physical traits and both natural and mental illnesses can be passed down from generation to generation through the blood line. Also, we have learned that behaviors and generational spiritual influences can also affect us both positively and negatively. Think about when a pregnant woman visits her physician's office for a routine checkup and is asked about her family's medical history. Her doctor may ask her if there's a history of heart disease, diabetes, high blood pressure or sickle cell anemia in the family because he understands if there is the unborn baby may also be subject to the same illnesses passed through the bloodline. He may also inquire of her previous pregnancies and deliveries to see if there are patterns that are concerning.

Such is the case concerning spiritual, mental and behavioral flaws and imperfections. Models tend to go through an entire family from generation to generation. If great grandmother was an alcoholic there's a good chance that grandmother will be too, then her daughter and so on. On a much larger scale, we see that an entire ethnic group can become predisposed to certain traits such as Sickle Cell Anemia among African Americans and Alcoholism among Native Americans.

Generational patterns can bring about bondage during an individual's life until that person addresses the thoughts and behaviors that caused the sin to take place. Some psychologists believe that behavior often exhibited is learned. Because of this, we often model and mirror coping mechanisms to issues and problems that arise in our lives. Based upon teachings displayed by our families, such as dealing with anger, communication, stress, finances, fornication, marriage, homosexuality, alcohol abuse, drug abuse, fear, anxiety, trust, physical abuse, molestation, prejudice, and even forgiveness.

If we have heard "what goes on in this house stays in this house" and to take family secrets to the grave then we are being taught to tell lies which can lead to developing feelings of shame. These secrets taint what we know and believe about ourselves and what to expect from our families and the world we live. We've been trained to reverence and remain loyal to those who have rule and authority over us and because of this we can sometimes find ourselves covering their secrets as we carry the burdens of their ugly truths while believing that we are protecting them in our silence.

If not addressed and dealt with these secrets can also unexpectedly resurface as we move through life forcing us to uncover something that was never meant to be covered in the first place.

Broken to be Made Whole

Imagine for a minute breaking a natural chain, specifically a bracelet if you will. It's made up of many links that are interconnected one to another. For that chain to become broken one single link has to come out of alignment with the other links. By doing so that one single link has the capability to change the functionality of the links before and after it. Once the single link becomes disconnected from the chain the chain as a whole is no longer completely functional.

Now consider the same concept when attempting to break chains of generational bondage in a family. The chain is comprised of family members, linked together one to another through the bloodline. For the generational bondage of that family to be broken, one family member has to come out of alignment with the practices and functions of the generations before it. Then unhealthy behavior(s) are no longer transmitted to the rest of the family, which will ultimately alter the destinies of the family members after it. However, this is a task easier said than done. The unique link that decides to break the chain that can change the sequence of the chain as a whole must be willing to sacrifice itself and be cut for the benefit of the whole. Are you ready to be broken so that others will be whole?

DC's Story

Energetic, smart, lover of music and basketball, handsome, gentle, kind and the apple of his father's and my eyes is how I would describe "DC" my then six-year-old son. His teachers often recognized him for his quick ability to learn and grasp information and for helping his classmates to learn too.

As full-time working parents on a limited income, DC's father and I would often need the help and support of our family to provide day care assistance for him while we were working during the summers. Being able to find a dependable family member that could consistently care for him during our working hours was a relief. We took DC to his house in the mornings, called to check on him during the day and picked him up after work. Initially, DC was excited for each visit with him; he played basketball with him; he went to the park with him, and he even allowed DC to splurge on snacks and goodies at the corner store.

At some point, things changed. DC started to complain each time we took him to his house. Often saying that he didn't want to go, confessing that he was mean to him. His dad and I ignorantly overlooked his requests, thinking that maybe it was just the "normal" picking behavior that men would do with young boys in an attempt to "harden" them that he disliked but unfortunate for DC we never asked him what "mean" meant and he never described it.

 It was now September; summer was over, and DC was back in school during the days. But the once energetic, eager to learn helper that the teachers all grown to know and love changed. Seemingly each day his dad and I were getting calls about his disruptive behavior. He was now acting out, talking back to teachers, picking fights with other classmates and hiding under tables. He was kicked out of three after-school programs because of his challenging and inappropriate behavior. At home, he would sometimes wet the bed, and cried at night when the lights in his room went out for bedtime.

One day while at the office, I received a call from a volunteer at his after-school program that told me I had to come pick DC up immediately. The staff expressed his troublesome behavior had reached a violent peak. Just minutes before her call to me DC slammed a nine-year- old boy's head into a brick wall in the cafeteria, and the young boy's head began to bleed profusely. Stunned, distraught and confused I left work and hastily made my way to the school to pick him up. Upon entering the school's office, I saw him sitting there dazed, a look that I've never seen him display before. In the other room was the nine-year-old boy sitting with his head wrapped in bandages next to his parents. I expressed my deepest and sincerest apologies to the young man and his parents then DC, and I made our way home. DC's dad and I sat down with him and attempted to find the answers to why DC would do something so traumatic and to gain some understanding of what was bothering him. But DC gave us no answers as he would just reply "nothing" and I was left feeling helpless in helping him. The next morning DC, his dad and I had a meeting with the school's principal, teacher and the school's psychologist. After reviewing all accounts of DC's past behavior during school his dad and I were encouraged to seek professional help for him. They insinuated that he could potentially have ADHD and perhaps we might be able to receive prescription meds to manage it. They further warned us that should DC's behavior persist he would be expelled and the incidences would go on his school record. Still confused and with no known motive behind his current behavior but knowing that this recommendation wasn't the best possible solution to whatever problem our son was facing we decided to take him out of the school and transfer him to another school. DC was now back in his old school, a Christian school. His dad and I made sure to make the school's personnel aware of his reason for leaving the previous school. In such a short time DC's behavior seemed to be back to normal, and all things were going well, and we were all pleased.

It was Valentine's Day, and DC's dad told him that he was taking him to the old sitter's house, and DC was ok with it. I was leery about keeping DC there, but seeing his face light up as he walked in the door to see his favorite male cousin there to play with and keep him company calmed my nerves. His dad and I went out for dinner, and as we were on our main course, we received a call and once again we were prompted to pick DC up. This time, it was because DC was found in the closet with his favorite cousin performing "bad touches." With my heart in the pit of my stomach, we grabbed for the check, and we swiftly made our way to the house. We arrived at the house snatched him, and we all made our way home. In the past, we've often talked to DC about and explained to him "good touch vs. bad touch." In disbelief, shocked and pained, on the way home DC's father and I began asking him "what happened in the closet and what made them do it?" While looking back at DC from the front passenger seat, I intensely awaited his response. The answer wasn't something that I anticipated. DC looked me in my eyes and with an elevated pitched voice DC told his father and me "uncle kissed my peepee." Immediately DC's dad and I faced one another, and while looking into one another's eyes, it was as if our souls departed our bodies then tears began to flow down our faces quickly. Those few five minutes of a car ride seemed like we were driving the hearse in a funeral processional while fighting beyond my emotions we made sure to console DC at that moment. Making certain to assure him that what his uncle did was wrong but that everything will be OK, and most importantly it wasn't his fault.

We finally arrived at home and DC's dad, and I began to shower DC with our love and affection. DC's father hugged and kissed him on his forehead and told me that he would be back later, and by looking at the anger in his eyes, I knew for certain where he was going.

One of the most fulfilling duties is that of a parent. On the other hand, one of the most difficult jobs is that of a parent. There's no how to parent for dummies book because not every parent and child are the same. As parents we are no longer solely judged by how we represent ourselves, we are also judged by the personal care and attention that is provided to our children. Holding DC in my arms that night I couldn't help but weep as I believed "I should've known better, and it was all my fault." I questioned "why didn't I see the signs." As a parent, I felt as if I failed my son. I should've known that no one awakens on a good morning and chooses to do wrong things.

Retrospectively taking a minute to think about things, I realized the strength and courage my son demonstrated by sharing his experience and standing in his truth. That's when I realized that my son was the link that sacrificed itself for the whole. He became broken so that those before him and after him might be whole. At that moment I promised to address and deal with my dark secrets that unexpectedly resurfaced as a result of my son's experience so that I can uncover something's in my life that was never meant to be covered in the first place.

I Cry For the Girl
Courtney Hawkins

I cry for the girl who's broken, battered, bloody and abused

I cry for the girl who's now confused

I cry for the girl who's lonely and empty inside

I cry for the girl who's so scared she hides

I cry for the girl who thinks it's her fault

Because her innocence is what you sought

I cry for the girl ashamed of her reflection

So she wears a mask to cover her imperfections

I cry for the girl who yearns for love so much

That she once welcomed your perverted touch

I cry for the girl who doesn't think that during her life she can make it

So she thinks of ways to take it

I cry for the girl who's bound and wants to be free

I cry for the girl who lives inside of me

Girls Don't Kiss Girls

"Now I lay me down to sleep, I pray thee Lord my soul to keep, if I should die before I wake, I pray thee Lord my soul to take, God bless mommy, daddy, and brother in Jesus name amen." At seven years old, this was the prayer that I prayed before going to sleep each night. Usually not too long after my head hit the pillow I was peacefully asleep but this night was different because I wasn't alone. The excitement of a girl's sleepover with my older cousin who was more like a big sister was well worth losing some sleep.

Even though it was dark and I couldn't see her face I could sense her proximity. She was lying in the twin bed across from mine in my room, and we stayed awake talking and giggling. In spite of how difficult it was to understand one another, we made sure to use our quietest whispering voice so that we wouldn't get caught staying up past our bedtime.

Suddenly the once muddled distant whisper of her voice became clearer as she was now cuddled next to me in my bed. My mother wouldn't dare allow someone to sit on the edge of my bed so her laying in my bed, under the covers was definitely against all the rules. Shocked that she had the audaciousness to defy my parent's authority I turned my face to her face as we laid next to each other. Breathing heavily with her mouth opened so that I could smell her breath, a smell so distinct that sometimes even now as an adult when I get a whiff of that unique smell breathed out by someone else's mouth it takes me back in time to her. Suddenly and without warning, she kissed me on my lips while her fingers searched and pinched at my flat, underdeveloped breast. My body went into a state of shock, and defenselessness and all my internal alarms went off knowing that this was the "bad touch" that I was warned about.

Good touches were reserved for mommies and daddies but she wasn't a mommy, and I wasn't a daddy. In mid-kiss my mother entered the room, flipped on the light and caught us. My mom began yelling as she spanked me with the belt simultaneously. With every firm tap of the belt to my bottom. She shouted out word by word "you (spank), should (spank), know (spank), better (spank), girls (spank), don't (spank), kiss (spank), girls (spank), that's (spank), nasty (spank)." Crying while trying to catch my breath with a sore behind I believed perhaps I should've known better, and maybe it's all my fault, and it could be she's right....I am nasty!

Her kiss wasn't the last kiss or touch, and over time as she became more experienced her kisses traveled from my lips to other parts of my body, and I was taught and encouraged to reciprocate it. As she and I grew "house" was the game we played when we were home alone. With my innocence taken and my identity stolen I was left behind questioning who I was. I was no longer the little seven-year-old girl, I became the "mommy", and she was the "daddy." I knew it was wrong, but there was no way that after kissing her again I could tell and risk the chance of getting spanked. I was confused and as perverted as the act was, each touch made me more comfortable and protected, favored and loved by her. Yet I was still embarrassed and guilt-ridden. After all "it's all my fault, I should've known better, girls don't kiss girls!"

Hide and Go Get It

Going to my best friend's house after school was always the highlight of my school week. It was always fun because she lived in a neighborhood where all of the popular kids lived and it was cool that they approved of me being a part of the crowd. Not to mention her house was the "fun" house since she seemingly had more freedom to do things than I did.

The school year had come to an end, and we were now the 8th- grade graduating class of '94. Without having to do too much convincing my mother and father allowed me to stay over at my best friend's house. While there a group of my 8th-grade friends and I decided to play a street game of hide-and-seek. Nothing and nowhere on the road was off limits, including an abandoned house. Some of us separated ourselves in teams attempting not to be sought by the one(s) who was it.

While running down the street trying to find a safe place to hide in unfamiliar territory he grabbed my hand and told me to come with him. I knew I could trust him because he was my cousin's cousin, so that made us cousins. I followed him as we ran into a garage and hid inside an old, dusty car with flat tires. He encouraged me to climb in the back seat so that we could lay flat and hide. That way we wouldn't be found by those that were trying to seek us. Thinking about how much it made sense I obliged his request, and I laid my body flat across the back seat of the car. Telling me that because the seat was so narrow, there wasn't enough room for him to fit by my side on the seat, therefore, he had to lay on top of me. With a smile on his face so big that I could see his pearly whites he told me to be calm and covered my mouth so that I couldn't make any sounds loud enough that would alert anyone of our whereabouts.

Feeling uncomfortable by the weight of his massive body on me I began to squirm and immediately as he released his hands he began to kiss me while putting his tongue in my mouth. He started to unbuckle his pants while I shook my head no trying to push him up off of me like I was lifting a heavy weight. Hide and seek swiftly turned to a game of hide and get it as my pants came down and he made three quick pumps inside of me.

A familiar voice called out my name, and I was startled and relieved. It was my best friend telling me that my parents were here to come and get me. Knowing that she was unable to see inside of the car he jumped off of me and quickly and discretely pulled up his pants as I did the same. With my best friend waiting, I made my way out of the car. I jumped in her arms, and while looking at me in my eyes, she noticed that something wasn't right so she asked me if I was ok, to which I hesitantly replied yes. I got in the car with my father, and I was mute as we drove home. Experience taught me not to kiss and tell and out of fear I was ready to keep the secret. Knowing that "I should've known better, it was my fault and again, I was nasty!"

2

COURT'S CASE

"Woman struck by vehicle dies of her injuries" is what the article in the police and courts section of the Buffalo News read on April 3, 2010. According to the article "an Amherst woman injured Sunday night when she was struck by a vehicle while crossing the street died Thursday.

The pedestrian was hit shortly before 8 pm Sunday by a car driven by Courtney Hawkins, 29, of North Tonawanda.

The Victim had been hospitalized in critical condition earlier this week in Erie County Medical Center's Trauma Intensive Care Unit with head, chest and leg injuries. Amherst police said investigators are still looking into the cause."

Sunday morning March 28, 2010, was as normal as the many Sunday's before. I woke up early with anticipation as I began to prepare my heart, mind, and body for the busy day ahead. Morning worship at the Tabernacle began at 10:00 am and evening worship was at 6:00 pm.

After a great morning worship celebration, I made my way back home to rest and relax before the evening service began. Once I was refueled and energized, I journeyed back to the tabernacle for the second portion of another fantastic service.

It was after 7 pm, and I was leaving the church, I ran to my car to avoid being soaked by the rain. When I got in the car, I called my son to tell him to prepare himself for my arrival. I picked him up from my mother's house around the corner, and we made our way home, this time taking an unusual route.

Journeying down the dark street at the recommended speed, with my wipers going I was given all green lights, so I continued to make my way down the road without interruption. While approaching an intersection, I began to see what appeared to be a red light. The combination of the rain hitting my window and the poorly lit street made my view blurred, and it was difficult for me to see where the light was coming from apparently. From afar I thought perhaps it was the reflection of something or maybe it was the taillight of another car. Whatever the red light was it didn't move. As I got closer to where the light was, it seemed to disappear.

Continuing at a steady speed, I crossed over the intersection. Then boom! Like the crash test dummy, my head quickly jerked back and forth, and the glass from my windshield shattered. I began shaking and screaming uncontrollably "Oh my God; I hit something." I swerved instantly to the right side of the road and parked my car diagonally. With my son still in the backseat, I immediately unrestrained myself and jumped out of the car. Looking ahead of me a nervous wreck, I didn't see anything. In slow motion, I hesitantly turned around, and that's when the red light reappeared on the road. Wearing a red coat, there she was laying in the street immobilized. The impact of the crash was so forceful that it made her hit my windshield, and she flew backward causing her to land on the ground. As two women ran towards me to console me, in complete shock I began screaming and crying repeatedly asking "What have I done? What have I done?" Standing there looking at her I wanted so badly for her to move, get up, and be ok.

Within minutes my Mother, Pastor, and First Lady were there. As the sirens became closer and closer, the once empty street became a cluttered crime scene as the crowd grew larger with police and spectators. The ambulance arrived and carefully took her away and soon after the crowd began to disappear. My mother took my son home with her and my pastor left shortly after.

It was my desire to go the hospital to make sure she was ok, but I was advised by the police to stay at the scene to wait until the on duty investigator arrived. As I sat in my First Lady's car waiting. It seemed like hours, sitting, waiting, and watching while the police began their investigation. They taped off the scene and even towed away my car for evidence.

Trying to comprehend what I did wrong, I began to reenact the accident in my mind. Inactive I was feeling intense hurt, fear, guilt, and shame. There were so many questions that I had… Was she ok? Was she at the hospital alone? What's taking the investigator so long? Why didn't I see her? And why did God allow this to happen? Even at that moment, my fragile mind was trying to conceive God's purpose in this.

The investigator arrived, came over and asked me to come to his car so that he could take my statement. With my First Lady by my side, sitting on the hard seats in the back of the patrol car giving my account of the accident made me a bit fearful. I began to consider "what if she's not ok?" Something about sitting there made me feel like a criminal. But that's not how the investigator treated me. To my surprise, he appeared very empathetic towards me. He shared how based upon my statement and my demeanor he felt that this was nothing more than an accident. After taking my statement, he gave me his card, told me that he would keep in touch and allowed my First Lady to take me home.

She took me home and once we arrived all I could think about was how I didn't want to be alone. She must've known I would feel this way because she invited me to stay at her home for the night. I quickly grabbed my clothes, and we made our way to her house. The usual fifteen-minute drive seemed like a slow eternity. Over the hours, it darkened outside and with every glaring red stop light, I would go into a trance as I thought about the "red light." Sirens flashed and dashed past us and I looked with my eyes fixated through the back glass doors of the ambulance wondering if it was her but knowing that it wasn't.

We arrived at the house and as we entered my Pastor was sitting there in the living room. Looking over past him on the other couch I noticed that he made up the couch for me with sheets and blankets to sleep. However, the softness and comfort of the sheets and blankets weren't enough to calm me or comfort me. I stayed awake that night staring, crying and shaking uncontrollably as I replayed the accident in my mind. Still wondering if she was ok?

The next few days were torture; I was on edge and every time the phone rang I thought it was the investigator with an update. I couldn't eat or sleep, and I was just an emotional wreck. Not fully capable of taking care of myself emotionally let alone my son, his father and I agreed that he would stay with him for some time as I spent the week at my Pastor and First Lady's house.

My only and constant concern was "How is she?" Finally, I received an update and was informed that she was in the hospital, in a drug induced coma with head, chest and leg injuries. My heart dropped, and something on the inside of me felt like this was the beginning of the end for her and me. I was still hopeful and prayerful that God could and would do the miraculous. Hearing the news and unable to be at her side, I felt like the black sheep of the family, wanting so desperately to be by her side, impatiently waiting for her to wake up. But the painful reality of knowing that I wouldn't be welcomed arose within. Nonetheless, something inside of me wanted to break all the rules and just follow my heart.

Saturday, six days later I attended our church's Community Impact Day. While there my Pastor called my First Lady and me into his office. He began to ask me "what are you doing after this?" "Are you coming over to our house?" Confused by the motive behind his questions I replied: "I'm not sure, why?" While reaching down to grab the Buffalo News paper he told me in a sympathetic and even-toned voice, "she died." In total disbelief, I read the article, and it read that she died two days before on Thursday. My heart dropped. I was afraid. Believing that the end was here, I started to think about the possibility of jail time. With confusion and fear in mind, I called the investigator to get some understanding of what was next?

While trying to face the reality of this loss, I became angry. I was angry because I thought about the "I should've," I should've gone to visit her and the regret I felt for not doing so. I felt that so many opportunities were taken from me. I missed the chance to slip in the back of the home going service and even the opportunity to know her.

No one told me about her, only her name. What I learned about her was from the Amherst Bee in the obituaries section. It was there, I was finally able to put a face to the "red light" and discovered that she was a mother of three daughters, five sisters, and a daughter of one surviving parent (mother). I learned that from Oct. 9, 1960-April 1, 2010 she liked being outdoors, where she enjoyed hiking, skiing, sewing, baking, bowling and how she always remembered and cherished her trips to France, Switzerland, and Hawaii.

Just like the black sheep, unlike the rest of the family I had no happy memories to comfort and console me as I mourned. Instead, I was left alone with only the painful and dreaded memories that caused feelings of guilt and shame so intense that it began to choke the life out of me.

Building a Case

"Police seek witnesses in pedestrian death" is what an April 7, 2010, article in the Amherst Bee read. According to the report, Senior Investigator for the Amherst Police is continuing the investigation and anyone who may have witnessed the incident is asked to call the Accident Investigation Unit.

My life as I knew it before March 28, 2010, at 8:00 pm was no longer the same. I was living in a new "normal." I was under investigation, and so was my friends and property. My car that was taken away that night was in police custody and remained there for over a month. While dismantling the car, it was found that my back breaks weren't in compliance with vehicle safety rules. After running my cell phone records, it was discovered by the investigators that I was having a conversation with my First Lady while driving the car before and at the time of the crash.

Charges

Much resembling the Snoop Dog song it seemed like "murder was the case that they gave me." I was obviously and painfully aware that there was a life lost and riddled with guilt. I felt that I was in part responsible for that outcome. However "Vehicular Manslaughter" was not something that my mind could wrap itself around. After all, it was an unfortunate tragic accident. There was no malicious intent, I had the right away, I wasn't under the influence of any drugs or substances, nor was I speeding in inclement weather but yet, unbeknownst to me, the very fact that my rear brakes were not in compliance was the one major factor that could have me behind bars facing jail time.

Soon it became the People of the State of New York VS. Courtney Hawkins. But it felt more like Satan vs. Courtney Hawkins. I was like Joshua in *(Zechariah 3:1-3) clothed* in filthy clothes, standing before the angel of the Lord, and Satan standing at his right hand to accuse him.

Standing in the courtroom in front of the judge as he read out loud all of the charges from the accident was hard to understand and hear because it was as if like an audible hallucination Satan was in my ear speaking louder. He recalled all of my past, when I; kissed a girl, when I was raped, when my son was molested, when I had sex before marriage and even when I killed her. That's when it became apparent… This case wasn't solely about the accident alone. I was standing trial for my life… Court's case!

3

BLACK DOES CRACK

Hide-and-seek or hide-and-go-seek is a children's game in which some players conceal themselves in the environment, to be found by one or more seekers. The game is played when one player, chosen at random (designated as being "it"), counts to a predetermined number while the other players hide. After reaching the number, the player who is "it" attempts to locate all concealed players.

In many ways, mental illness in the African American community mirrors elements found in this game. This chapter, Black Does Crack outlines some of the cultural and societal factors which come into play in perpetuating the prevalence of mental illness in African American communities.

Consider this parallel: have you ever been in a dark place in your life where you felt so alone that you secluded and hid amongst the ruins and debris of your circumstances? You were too weak or embarrassed to vocally scream for help but deep down you wished that someone, anyone would hear your silent screams for help, and at times, desperately wanting and waiting for someone to just find you where you were and save you.

Based on information gathered from the "African American Community Mental Health Fact Sheet" from the National Alliance on Mental Illness and from "African American Communities and Mental Health" from Mental Health America. Researchers have stated that mental illness in the African American community is at disproportionate levels in relation to the wider population. Unfortunately, one of the primary sources of strength found in this community–the church, can also be a primary source of pain when it comes to mental illness.

In the African American community, biases based on culture against mental health professionals in particular, and health care professionals in general, prevent many who could benefit from accessing care in seeking the support that is available. These biases stem from prior personal, as well as anecdotal, experiences which have often resulted in historical misdiagnoses, inadequate treatment, and a lack of cultural understanding.

In addition to the biases that exist in the African American community, because of other factors (which are beyond the scope of this book and chapter), there are very few Africa American professionals that can help when someone from our culture needs support. Only 2% of psychiatrists, 2% of psychologists and 4% of social workers in the U.S. are African American. Resulting not only in a lack of providers but also in a lack of research done that challenges the available information regarding mental illness–most of which has been normed on white males and doesn't take into account the lives and experiences of women, African Americans nor other people of color.

If and when they reach out, rather than relying on traditional health care professionals, regardless of how prudent it might be to go to these professionals; African Americans typically rely on family, religious and social communities for emotional support. However, the catch-22 here is that mental illness is frequently stigmatized, misunderstood and even ridiculed in the African-American community. If the church's mission is to provide answers to humanity's problems that lead to abundant living but we don't see or understand mental illness (depression, bipolar, anxiety, and suicide) as a problem then how can we provide the answers?

In addition to the social and cultural stigmas, African Americans are often at a socioeconomic disadvantage in terms of accessing both medical and mental health care and those living below the poverty line are two to three times more likely to report severe psychological distress than those living above the poverty threshold. High numbers of African Americans are uninsured and underinsured yet they are 20 percent more likely to report serious psychological distress than their white counterparts.

Research states that African American adults are more likely to have feelings of sadness, hopelessness, and worthlessness than are adult whites; and while African Americans are less likely than whites to die from suicide as teenagers, African American teenagers are more likely to attempt suicide than are white teens (8.2 percent v. 6.3 percent).

African Americans of all ages are more liable to be victims of serious violent crime than are non-Hispanic whites, making them more likely to meet the diagnostic criteria for post-traumatic stress disorder (PTSD).

African Americans were more likely to believe that depression was "normal" than the overall survey average. 56 percent believed that depression was a normal part of aging; 45 percent believed it was normal for a mother to feel depressed for at least two weeks after giving birth; 40 percent thought it was normal for a husband or wife to feel depressed for more than a year after the death of a spouse.

Some barriers to the treatment of depression cited by African Americans included: denial (40 percent), embarrassment/shame (38 percent), don't want/refuse help (31 percent), insufficient financial resources/insurance (29 percent), fear (17 percent), lack of knowledge of available treatments and/or problems (17 percent) and an acceptance of hopelessness (12 percent). Because of cultural and societal conditioning, 63 percent of African Americans believe that depression is a personal weakness.

Research further states that African Americans are less likely to take an antidepressant for treatment of depression: only 34 percent take one even when it is prescribed by a doctor.

My Story

Although I felt as though I've known depression most of my life I was informally introduced to depression through Zoloft when I was 17 years old while sitting with my mother in the family room watching "All My Children", a soap opera. During the break, Zoloft appeared and spoke to me and compassionately asked me "Have you felt the weight of sadness? Have you felt exhausted, hopeless, anxious, and whatever you do you still feel lonely? If so you may be experiencing depression; a medical condition affecting over twenty million Americans." Zoloft told me that depression causes were unknown but that it may be a result of an imbalance of natural chemicals between nerve cells in my brain. Zoloft gave me hope that they could/would help me fight depression to correct this imbalance. Knowing that I was in an unhealthy relationship with depression. I instantly felt supported and comforted when Zoloft told I that I should no longer allow depression to make me feel this way anymore, but then I reversely felt abandoned when they said the catch was I had to talk to my doctor first because only they could diagnose depression. Zoloft made many more attempts over the years to communicate with me and continued to reassure me that they could help. I never accepted their relief because there was no way that I could tell my doctor that I knew depression personally. It felt like telling someone for the first time that you were in a physically abusive relationship. I was just too embarrassed and afraid.

During my late teens, I often felt sad, anxious, lonely and empty but I could not understand why or pinpoint any definite reason for these feelings which often exacerbated my sense of irritability and hopelessness. The facts that I had been molested, sexually mistreated and neglected weren't things that came to mind at the time as possible causes for why I became to know depression so intimately. So with no particular purpose in mind, I began to think perhaps I was just another emotional woman whose time of the month was approaching. I learned at the age of thirteen that when a young girl entered into womanhood that at least once a month for three to seven days she could use her menstrual cycle as an excuse for why her emotions were imbalanced or uncontrollable.

Then there was the accident. After the accident had occurred, there were plenty of times when my emotions were like an emotional rollercoaster. Some days I was not extremely high, but I was "okay." Then there were other times when I was extremely low, times when I was too scared to go home, times when I was too depressed to get dressed, times when I was too afraid to be alone and times when I just wanted to hide from the world. Whether it was me driving down the dark street or whether it was the sound of rain hitting my windowpane any little thing seemingly sparked a change in my attitude for the worst.

Often, I only wanted to be alone. Holidays were stressful; Labor Day, Veteran's Day, It didn't quite matter. However, Mother's Day and Christmas were probably the two worst holidays. I avoided family gatherings out of guilt and punishment because I told myself I didn't deserve to celebrate the holidays. Who was I to have the privilege to honor my family and be happy because she's not here to celebrate with hers is what I told myself? "Who am I to celebrate motherhood when I took someone else's mother away?"

I felt alone; like no one understood how I felt, to be honest, there were times I didn't fully comprehend my feelings. How is it possible to grieve this loss? I'm not her family. I'm the person that committed this crime.

I'm the person that caused the pain for her family who's now left behind to mourn her. So will anyone understand that I'm grieving? Is it okay that I grieve? I never even met her. In my head, I knew that I don't have control over life and death. I knew that's something that's only in God's hands, but you couldn't tell my heart that at the time. My grief was a result of a broken heart, not a broken brain. All efforts to heal my heart with the head failed. Most of the comments that I heard following my loss, while intellectually accurate, were emotionally barren.

I awakened early one morning, wiped my eyes and as I usually do I reached over to grab my phone to tell Facebook what was on my mind which is usually "Good Morning New Mercies! Hello, Grace! Greetings Purpose!" It's my way of telling God and reminding others that I'm grateful for a new day. It had been a while since I took the time out to tell God thank you even though the Bible tells us that in everything we should give Him thanks. I guess everything that happened earlier that week had caught up to me, and thankful for feeling abandoned, hurt and afraid wasn't the word I would use to best describe my attitude. Friday night depression crept upon me; I wrestled with suicidal thoughts that attempted to convince me to crash into a wall on the expressway and kill myself. Not to mention the motherlode of all anxiety attacks had gripped me to the point that I cried myself to sleep. As I aroused Saturday morning, I began to cry as I immediately thought about the few short hours before. Throughout that day I found comfort in my sorrow and my face was cleansed by my continual flow of tears that covered my face.

To my surprise Sunday was a new day filled with new hope. I woke up refreshed, and I was thankful for it. Sunday's were my favorite day of the week. It was like my regularly scheduled therapy session. I often left feeling prepared to conquer the world until I got to the parking lot and the devil seemingly quickly came to steal the seed that was planted in me. I remember this particular Sunday morning entering into the tabernacle just as (*Psalm 100*) declares; I entered his gates with thanksgiving and his court's with praise; I gave thanks to him and praised his name. I walked down the aisle and made my way to my reserved seat which was on the first row directly across from the pulpit. As the praise team sang joyful songs, I stood with a spirit of gladness as I joined in worship for a while to my Lord with the clapping of my hands.

Then all of a sudden like a dark cloud hovering over a bright day I immediately took my seat as confusion and anger overtook me. I went from being in a room filled with people listening to joyful noise to feeling alone in a quiet room of one upset with God. I started to reason in my mind. An inner debate with Him began about why didn't He tell me…why did He allow me to go…why did the Holy Spirit, that I know I hear, that speaks to me, that I listen to and at times I abide by, not warn me of the dangers ahead, to not go down this street and take this way home that particular day? I was angry because there were answers I didn't have at that moment and still don't totally have to this day.

Seated on the pulpit was my First Lady. She must have noticed that something wasn't right with me because immediately after church she had spoken to one of the ministers and asked her if she could talk to me. At the end of the service the minister came to me and asked me if I was okay and what was going on? So I truthfully told her that I was upset with God, and I began to tell her why. I remember her telling me that one couldn't be upset with God; that I can't question God; that I was supposed to have faith. Immediately I became infuriated. I'm a believer that believes that I can ask God and that He can handle all of me, even at that moment. The Bible says "Be angry but sin not" and I didn't commit any offense that I was aware of. My anger resulted from hurt. From not understanding why did I have to go through what I went through and why she wasn't here. From the time the accident occurred until the time she passed away I was praying, seeking God and I believed in her full recovery. Others would tell me that they envisioned her coming to our church, and she was praising God, and I choose to believe that. Yet that's not what happened.

After that talk, I shut down all the more, thinking, no one understands. There were days before that, and there were days after that I was upset with God because he wouldn't answer my "why?" When those feelings would resurface, I wouldn't tell anyone. Or at least I knew not to say it to that minister.

Some days were completely horrible to the point where I sat in the church and felt like I wanted to kill myself right there and then. I can recall another Sunday sitting in the back of the church in the midst of an excellent service, and while I was sitting there again, seemingly all of a sudden, out of nowhere, anger, hurt and despair overtook me and once again I was reminded of her and the accident. Feeling overwhelmed with anxiety I began crying so loudly within myself. I wanted to go to the altar and receive prayer, but the stigma of being a minister in the church and going to receive prayer hit me. I thought, "Okay, how many times are you going to go up for prayer about this thing? Shouldn't you be healed? Shouldn't you be delivered from it?" What is it going to look like to others who are in the congregation if they continually see a minister going up for prayer? Why would they want to receive prayer from someone who's seemingly always going through something? So that stigma caused me to take a back seat. I told myself that if I did not receive a hug from anyone in that church before I left that once, I left I was going to kill myself. So vulnerable and wanting an embrace so badly I was even willing to go to "that" minister. I just wanted to lay my head on her lap and cry. Well, fear paralyzed me, and I didn't move nor did I receive an embrace.

I didn't want them to answer the why for me. I just simply wanted someone there to give me a hug. I wanted someone to see past what they thought to be this hard, well put together exterior. I wanted them to see past what was seemingly this standoffish woman because if they got past their perceptions of my exterior, they would have known that I was insecure and that I didn't love or value myself. They would have known that there was a little girl on the inside of me that was crying out to be loved and validated.

After service, on the ride home with my friend I shut down and became quiet as I often did when depression would visit me. When asked if I was OK? I would often respond yes, I'm OK knowing that my ok was inside of me being brOKen.

The next Sunday, my emotional roller-coaster had me "waaaaaay up I felt blessed." I was happy, and the smile on my face showed it. After service one of the sisters came to me with a big smile on her face as she hugged me confidently saying, "God told me to give you a hug." My smile was turned upside down as I stood in disbelief letting her hug me. In my mind, I was thinking to myself, "God probably did tell you to embrace me, but it wasn't today, it was last week."

Just thinking about that situation has helped me personally to become more obedient to the voice of God. If I was alone, the week before the chances of me following through with my suicide attempt had a great possibility of happening. That particular experience allowed me to see how vital it is to move when God tells us to go because literally, someone's life may be depending upon it.

I think about the people who come to church because they're told that the church provides answers to their problems. I believe this to be true, but if the church isn't prepared to know the difference between a person's personality and a person's mental illness, to know what depression looks like. What bipolar looks like. What schizophrenia looks like. What an anxiety attack vs. a heart attack looks like. To learn that these are real diagnosable illnesses just like cancer is. Just like high blood pressure is. Just like diabetes is. If we are not well equipped to deal with these issues or to even recognize that there is a problem; instead telling these seekers, "Just have faith." and "What do you mean you're depressed, just have faith." How can we effectively help and meet the needs of the people?

If society can understand and accept that an individual can go to war and because of their traumatic experience be diagnosed with post-traumatic stress disorder and if needed receive prescribed medication to manage their illness. Why is it not okay that I was in an accident, and as a result of my experience I was diagnosed with PTSD and depression, and if I did get to the point where I sought a pill to manage the illness, then it's okay just like someone with high blood pressure and diabetes. God did say, He's able to heal all matter of sickness and disease.

We've all heard the saying "Black Don't Crack" It usually refers to the skin of African Americans not wrinkling or reflecting their real age as much as individuals from other ethnic backgrounds. It also speaks to the stereotype of the strong black community that leads many African Americans especially women to believe that they don't have the indulgence or time to experience depression. Black women for decades are seen as unshakeable, incontrovertible and naturally durable, not cracking under pressure.

"Black Does Crack" when our burdens become too heavy for us to handle alone we do crack under pressure, we do suffer from mental illness and yes, we do contemplate and commit suicide.

Karyn's Story

Karyn Washington, the beautiful visionary behind the encouraging and uplifting website, Forbrowngirls.com. Karyn created the forum to celebrate the beauty of darker shades of brown skin, to encourage women to embrace the skin they're in.

At just the age of 22, while finding it difficult to grieve the loss of her mother Karyn committed suicide.

Karyn's empowering plea on her Forbrowngirls.com site read "As humans, regardless of color, age, socio-economic status, gender, and other characteristics, we MUST build each other up rather than tear each other down in order to change the world and create a better place for our children and future generations. As women, it is imperative as well as our duty to love ourselves unconditionally, smile and laugh often, and NEVER allow ANYONE to steal our joy."

What I find most important to remember about Karyn's story is that a woman who dedicated her life to encourage and inspire others also lacked the same encouragement and inspiration needed for herself during one of her most difficult times. One would assume that a smile assures happiness and strength, but it doesn't. Being strong isn't smiling when you should be crying. It's finding the courage to cry in front of a world that tells you that you should be smiling instead.

So who or what stole Karyn's Joy? Was it her grief? I wish I could've told her the answer, which was there's an adversary whose sole focus was to steal, kill and destroy the joy that she wanted so desperately to safeguard even in the midst of her grief.

According to the Grief Recovery Method; the majority of incorrect beliefs about dealing with a loss can be summed up in six myths.

- *Time heals all wounds*

- *Grieve alone*

- *Be strong*

- *Don't feel bad*

- *Replace the loss*

- *Keep busy*

I wish I could've helped her to correct her beliefs surrounding those myths. I would've told her that the reality is *(John 10:10)* says *"I am come that they might have life and that they might have it more abundantly."* I would've reminded her that *(Ecclesiastes 3:14)* says *"There is a time to weep, and a time to laugh; a time to mourn and a time to dance."* I wish I could've taken her to *(Nehemiah 8:10)* and showed her that *"the Joy of the Lord is her strength."* I would've assured her that she could lean on me for her life, health, and strength but since I can't tell her these things, let me remind you.

If you are feeling heartbroken or experiencing grief of any loss, there is hope.

- *(Psalm 34:18)* *"The Lord is nigh unto them that are of a broken heart; and saveth such as be of a contrite spirit."*

- *(Isaiah 26:3)* *"Thou wilt keep him in perfect peace, whose mind is stayed on thee because he trusteth in thee."*

- *(Psalm 30:5)* *"Weeping may endure for a night, but joy cometh in the morning."*

- *(Matthew 11:28)* *"Come unto me all ye that labour and are heavy laden and I will give you rest."*

**Remember, if you or someone you know is having suicidal thoughts or feelings, you must seek help immediately. **

4

THE MASTER OF DISGUISE

We've heard it said, "You don't get a second chance to make a first impression." Rather it's during a job interview or meeting someone that you are romantically interested in for the first time. Often it is our "Image consultants" that they are introduced to. For many of us being totally transparent and forthcoming with negative traits that are a part of our character and habits that are not so attractive can be both frightening and a bit intimidating. So instead we choose to present ourselves leading with the most appealing and interested attributes first. This can be a bit misleading, but the fear of being discovered is worth the risk. We don't believe that if they are sincerely interested in building something with you, they will be willing to accept all facets of you.

Image consultants much like make-up artists can serve as paid representatives who mask the imperfections of others. They are professionals who assess the current status of the public's perception of an individual, company, or other organization. Their purpose is to evaluate the degree of positive and negative opinions present and determine the best way to enhance the positive aspects of the public image.

Have you ever thought about what message your style of clothing is revealing and what it says about you? As individuals, clothing and appearance are some of the most powerful and important ways we have of expressing ourselves, our values and our attitudes. The way a musician uses instruments and words to express themselves through a song and the way an artist can create a masterpiece with splashes of paint on an empty canvas is the same way in which we use our clothing to creatively express ourselves for the world to see. It can be displayed in loud, vibrant colors, leopard prints and horizontal stripes, blazers, and jeans, miniskirts with off the shoulder tops or long flowing dresses made by high-end designers. Style is an individualistic form of self-expression. It is self–knowledge and self-confidence displayed through what we choose to wear on any particular day.

Many of us may know what message we are sending or perhaps we are naïve to that communication having become so influenced by our culture and the latest trends that we don't know any other way to think about clothing. Our fundamental beliefs around what we should or shouldn't be or do are formulated by Family, Religion, Friends and Media. External messages can have a powerful influence on the development of our beliefs and personal standards. It can become easy to neglect the qualities and values that make you an individual in an effort to conform to widespread society.

Our choices are often dictated by these social expectations that don't always connect with who we are as individuals. We tend to feel an overwhelming amount of pressure to be liked, admired and fit in at any cost. That message is translated in magazines, commercials and fashion shows. It is the topic of discussion among women and men, boys and girls in the office, schools, beauty salons, barber shops and malls all across America. We live in a society where the money we possess carries more value than our individual morals and ethics.

We are often categorized based upon our material possessions and how much money they cost believing that the more expensive the item, the more valuable it converts to us and others. Purchasing designer labels with the hope that possession of the piece somehow signifies that we are no longer worthless. For some "Keeping up with the Joneses" becomes something to endeavor towards at any cost even if it means to live beyond your means. Now I'm not saying that you should go and abandon all of your fine quality possessions and live a modest lifestyle. If this is your preference and you can financially support beautiful quality belongings by all means do so. God wants us to have nice things. However, the problem exists when there are individuals that are living outside of their means, hiding behind masks to impress others. Some people are walking around showcasing some of the classiest shoes and purses in their collections from the most recognizable designers that will cause any onlooker to become envious all while hiding the fact that they are unable to pay their bills in full and support their families "Robbing Peter to support Paul." While others do great jobs of dressing up their outer appearance making it look as if that they have it all together but if you took a peek into their personal lives you'll find that it's in disarray.

Some things aren't always what they appear to be. A "knock-off" even resembles the real thing. We assume just because it or they have what we see as a high price tag (teacher, preacher, artist, entertainer, athlete, doctor, lawyer, etc.) we are certain to get something of quality and authenticity. To find out if it's genuine, you need to get close enough to the thing you're interested in to check for any defects. In doing so, you may find that it looks good but may not be authentic or void of deficiencies.

My Closet

On the outside, it looked as if I had it all together but if you took a look into my closet, you would've noticed that I was living in complete dysfunction. It's common for us to hear about someone abusing sex, drugs or alcohol when they're attempting to disguise their pain and avoid problems but for me, I chose to dress to impress especially on Sunday's. One day without hesitation God told me "You're a beautifully wrapped package but empty inside." My low self-esteem and depression at the time lead me to turn to material things and even form fitting clothes to fill my sense of void and empty identity. I guess I was in search for affection and comfort while attempting to display perfectionism. Since my identity was stolen, I purchased, hid behind and proudly adorned myself with the renowned names of Tiffany, Michael Kors, Movado, Prada, BCBG, Jimmy Choo, Chanel, Marc Jacobs and others hoping that their names will add value to me because I didn't realize the value in adoring Courtney.

The consequences of my oniomania were devastating and embarrassing. There were times when my depression and low self-esteem would create impulses that caused me to neglect my financial responsibilities which produced insurance lapses, car repossessions, and shut offs not to mention how I robbed God in my tithes and offerings. On one occasion I had to go to my employer and ask for an advance in pay because my car was repossessed the night before as my son and I was lying in my room watching TV. At around 9:00 pm we heard a loud beeping noise outside of our window much similar to that of a garbage truck. Confused by the sound and the time of day, I went to my window to see where the noise was coming from that's when I realized that my car was being confiscated. My heart began to immediately pound faster and faster as I quickly grabbed my shoes, ran down the stairs to go outside in just enough time to get the essential items from my car. As my son looked from the bedroom window, I can only imagine what he felt as I tried to reassure him that everything would work out. Fortunately it did work out, but unfortunately, that wasn't the first time or the last time he witnessed something being taken away or came home to something being shut off. The all-time low was when my insurance lapsed a year after that. I had to take my car off the road for two weeks. I needed to go to one of my sisters in the church and rent her car. Too embarrassed to tell my son why I had Sister Nikki's car I said to him that our car was in the shop getting work done and I was borrowing hers.

Spring Cleaning

If you require any detailed and intricate details about a creation, ask the creator, not the image consultant. It's their job to represent the creation for their gain. They're not always honest and accurate and often it's because they lack the detailed knowledge of the design because they didn't create it. However, the creator knows all about the intricate details that make up the product and its deficiencies. When needed, it's the Manufacturer of the creation that will do a recall to improve the production and eliminate the insufficiencies that hinder the creation's ability to perform the way it was purposed to.

One day while doing some spring cleaning in my house God lead me to my clothes closet while cleaning my closet He instructed me on how to clean up those secret, closeted places in my life.

Here's what He said;

I must be willing to do the work. *(James 2:26) "Faith without works is dead being alone."* I couldn't say that I wanted things in my life to change, expect God to do his part, while I sat around not doing the work necessary for it to change.

Get rid of things that I don't need and that I've outgrown. I had to be willing to let go of people, places and things that hindered my progression and no longer served me. There were times that I would hoard and hold on to certain items because of the memories attached to it. For me throwing away the object somehow meant I was throwing away the experience. Doing that terrified me. I had to ask myself "WTF" Courtney? I needed to be clear on What's The Function behind this item? I also needed to take inventory of my personal relationships and one by one ask myself and God, have I outgrown them? If so, I needed to give them up and move on.

Put things that I need in their proper places and take good care of them. (Prioritize things and people). I take pride in the fact that I'm a loyal, supportive and trustworthy friend. Often my need to please, care for and support my friendships often meant neglecting me, my responsibilities and even my relationship with God. I had to become clear on who and what things were most important and prioritize those people, places, and things.

Don't hide the stained clothing in the back. I had to stop hiding in the background of others because I was too embarrassed by my stains and flaws. I had to know and believe that the blood of Jesus was able to cleanse each one of my stains, and there was no reason for me to hide.

Give some things away. I had to learn it's OK for me to give pieces of myself away to others. To have wisdom on when to share parts of my time etc. with others. To use discernment on what parts of my testimony to tell, understanding that you can't tell everyone everything because they may not be able to fit or "walk in your shoes."

Lose some weight. There were some things which God wouldn't allow me to get rid of. For me to adequately fit back into some imperative things I needed to lose some of the physical and mental "weight and baggage" I've gained over the years. I had to shed fear, shame, inadequacy and guilt because those weights were hindering me from operating in my greater purpose.

Remember why I purchased it. If it weren't special, I wouldn't have purchased it. The same way we buy clothing because of our like for it and the belief that what we purchased would serve a purpose was the same reason Jesus, with his blood, "purchased us with a purpose."

Order, Organize, and Cleanout! As often as I need to, it's important for me to bring order to those areas of my life that seem hectic. Organize and prioritize those people, places, and things and when necessary clean out those dirty, closeted areas of my life that only hinder me from being the best me. Knowing that God can create in me a clean heart and renew in me the right spirit.

My thinking was so disordered; I believed that putting on designer labels would in some way make me feel better about myself when I was weak and that Tiffany, Michael, Jimmy and Marc would help me fight this battle in my mind. I was looking for external solutions to fix an internal problem. God had to remind me that I was wearing the wrong things and fighting the wrong battle. Therefore, to be strong, I had to put on the full armor of God. The belt of truth buckled around my waist, the breastplate of righteousness, and my feet fitted with the readiness that comes from the gospel of peace; also taking up my shield of faith, the helmet of salvation and the sword of the spirit.

He had to remind me of who I was; a designer's original, custom fitted with a purpose, a Virtuous woman, clothed with strength and dignity, who laughs without fear of the future. When I speak, my words are wise, and when I give instructions, it's with kindness.

We've heard "when you look good you feel good" however, could it be the opposite? When you feel good, you look good? What you are wearing and how you are wearing it says a lot about you, how you feel, which parts of your body you like and dislike and how confident you are. Self-esteem is an individual's reputation with themselves and is comprised of two things; Self-Confidence and Self-Respect. It's important to remember that being sexy is not found in a particular dress, but rather from a confidence that exudes from the inside of you. You make the clothing attractive. Have you ever seen two people wearing the same outfit but for some reason, it looks better on one and not the other? Could it be that one was adorned with self-confidence and respect which caused the outfit to pop and the other did not? Nowadays we call that "Swag" but years from now it will still be considered self-confidence. When we don't esteem ourselves, it doesn't matter what label or hair style we wear it will only temporarily fool ourselves and others of how we really feel about ourselves inwardly. When you know who you are, feel good and positively support yourself you will become attractive to yourself and others.

It is important to be mindful of the messages your clothing is conveying to the world. Ask yourself am I representing myself in the best way possible? Does my attire clearly display the attitudes and personal standards I have for myself or are you even aware of your personal standards because for so long you have conformed to the beliefs and criteria of those around you? If this is the case then perhaps you need to take the time to get to know who you are and reevaluate if you agree with those "shoulds" that were placed on you by others. Once you do this, it will make the clothing selection process much more meaningful and authentic. Because then you won't feel pressured to put together an outfit based upon trends or the name brand labels of others but instead you'll comfortably clothe yourself with self-confidence, respect, strength, and dignity which will cause others to label you as virtuous.

5

<u>ADDICTED TO LOVE</u>

Love is patient, love is kind, it's not envious, it's not boastful, it's not proud, it's not rude, it's not self-seeking, it's not easily angered, it keeps no record of wrong. Love delights in the truth, it protects, it trusts, hopes and preserves. Love covers, love gives, love is life, love is work, love transforms, love is contagious, love is wise, love is a gift, love is fearless, love is infinite, love is eternal, love never fails, love is addictive, and I'm addicted to love!

Perfect Fit

I believed only once in a lifetime will you truly find your perfect fit, a soul mate that you connect with mind, body and spirit. The special someone who makes you feel alive when you were dying inside. That person who teaches you how to love, live and laugh because with them life is worth living. That one true love that turned your life right side up when it was upside down for so long. You tell them things that you've never shared with anyone else, and they absorb everything you say and are interested in hearing more. You share your hopes and aspirations for the future, visions that you pray will come true, dreams that haven't yet manifested and the many disappointments life has dealt you. When beautiful and amazing things happen they're the first to know because you're confident that they will share your excitement. They are not ashamed to cry with you in bad times and laugh and celebrate with you when things turn around for your good. They never make you feel like you're less than the best, but instead, they make you feel like you're more than enough. They are not interested in building you up to break you down; instead, they gather your broken pieces to help rebuild you stronger than you were before. You love for them to come around but hate for them to leave. There's never any awkward silence or any need for unceasing conversation because your love for one another speaks volumes even in the quiet calmness found in their presence. You can confidently and comfortably remove your mask and be seen by them knowing that they love you, flaws and all. The things that seem insignificant to most people such as a simple touch, eye contact and a tight embrace become priceless treasures locked in your lover's heart endlessly. Mornings are brighter, smiles are wider, and laughs are louder. Hearing their voice brings peace during a raging storm. Good morning and good night texts become more significant because you understand that you're the first person on their mind as they arise and the last one they think of before the lie down to sleep. The simplest things cause flashbacks of them like the taste of a chocolate Reese's cup, the smell of rain or even a gentle summer's breeze. You're vulnerable with them and one by one you knock down all of your walls that once kept guard over your heart. Because you know that one day it may be broken, you discover that being vulnerable is the only way to experience the pure pleasure of love, and you allow yourself to trust, as you close your eyes and fall head over heels in love. Tranquil peace and strength are discovered when you realize that the one you love genuinely and unconditionally loves you back.

I found that perfect fit, but it wasn't the perfect time. I wasn't his, and he couldn't be mine, I fell for his wit, intelligence, his passion for fulfilling a higher purpose, a heart that was made of gold and a smile that brightened any dark place. I met him during a time when I was most vulnerable; my heart was wide open, and I was learning how to love and value myself all over again. I was more concerned and leery of other diversions, but he told me that he was the one I should be worried about. I didn't understand at the time the truth and the weight of his statement. He immediately captivated me, stole my heart and I became addicted to his love. He was the oval peg that I tried to force fit inside of a circle no matter how much I knew it wouldn't fit seamlessly. If loving him was wrong I didn't want to be right, if being right meant living without him I was willing to love him all my life. He was my little secret that only my heart and friend Nita knew of. She and I would talk about him often late at night, early mornings and sometimes during the day. The one that cried with me when I spoke to her about my love for him. Nita told me that she understood how it felt to want someone so much that it made you cry. She knew how it felt to get excited at the sound of their voice and in their presence so much so that you become immobilized. I never knew a love like this before; it was incredible. It was a love connection so powerful and electrifying that it often shocked even me. His love was like a drug that kept me high on cloud nine, and whenever I would feel down, I would medicate with his love potion number nine.

Crazy in love is what I felt when reality set in reminding me once again that he was the perfect fit, but it wasn't the right time. I wasn't his, and he couldn't be mine. Maybe in a past life, I was his wife or could it be that we were never really meant to be? I asked myself was I so addicted to the pain of loving someone so non-attainable. As wrong as I knew it was to love him I couldn't let him go. I tried, and I cried, fasted and prayed, tried many times to go our separate ways. My spirit was willing, but the soul tie was so strong it made my flesh weak. I tried to speak those things that are not as though they were but it was hard to convince myself that I didn't have feelings for my perfect sir. He was one of a kind, but again he couldn't be mine, at least not during that space in time.

What If

Trying to answer the question "What if" can have you doing things and going places you never imagined venturing. For me the question "What if?" meant traveling to see Houston for an answer.

One day while out enjoying lunch I received a friend request on Facebook from an old acquaintance. It had been over ten years since I last seen him. As I accepted his request, I immediately went back in time and began to recall the memories we once shared together. We were both young; he was handsome and funny, I had a child, he had none, we were both fresh out of relationships, he was ready and willing to be together, but I wasn't because of "What if?" What if I'm meant to be with my son's father? What if Houston was the one? What if Houston wasn't the one? There were so many things to consider, and ultimately I chose my family which meant reconciling with my son's father. I reluctantly said my goodbyes to Houston, and he quickly vanished without a trace. I often wondered about him over the years like where he was and who was he with? Was he wondering about me as much as I wondered about him? As I browsed through his profile in an attempt to become reacquainted with him so many unanswered questions were answered. I learned that he relocated to Houston and was newly married with two children. Looking through his pictures was like being told his new life in a thousand words. He appeared happily in love. I must admit it made me a bit sad as "What if?" reared its ugly head again. Periodically we in boxed one another to catch up and the more we caught up it seemed like we were getting caught up in the feelings that once were. He shared how he often thought of me over the years and his many attempts to find me. He was excited that he found me and my heart echoed those same feelings. He opened his heart and revealed how I was the love interest in his BET movie; you know the story of the one who got away and reappeared causing the main character to question his feelings for two women. This was flattering for me to hear; after all, I was single and completely frustrated at the time. I was upset because cupid's arrow seemed to hit everyone but me accurately. Even though he was married and hearing him express his feelings for me after all these years was so wrong something about it inside of me felt so right. Perhaps it was my need to feed/boost my ego or maybe it was the beginning of my "What if?"

After some time he extended to me the invitation of an all-expense paid trip to visit him in Houston. He told me to look at it as two friends catching up, but everything within me knew that it was much more than that. Even though the thought of what if made me weak ultimately my convictions were stronger and I declined his offer after all, I'm not just single I'm a saved woman of God with a purpose to empower and unite woman. The unpleasant memories of my past unfaithful relationship flooded my mind, and I thought there was no way that I could intentionally agree to secretly visit and spend quality time with another woman's husband. There was no way that I could demoralize myself and compromise my beliefs and standards. There was no way that I could look my little sister in the face and become that do as I say not as I do mentor. There was too much to lose, and nothing to gain is what I repeatedly told myself in an attempt to do the right thing. I continued this self-recording in my mind in an effort to do the right thing, and whenever the thought of taking him up on his offer would arise, I would press play.

Vulnerability crept upon me again, and frustration caused me to break the motivational recording I once played. I began to tell God that I didn't want to be single. To which He replied "Not yet and what's for you will not pass you" needless to say that wasn't the response I desired to hear. I questioned why God would allow him to reappear in my life after all of these years. I knew He wasn't sending me a husband who's someone else's husband. Was this some pop quiz that the devil sought permission from God to test me on? With that in mind, I decided to do some studying so that I could be prepared spiritually for this test. I downloaded Juanita Bynum's "No More Sheets" and while watching and listening attentively, I took notes on how to rid myself of the soul ties that I obviously still had with him. The reason for the pop quiz suddenly became apparent. For me to become completely available for my husband, I had to take care of some unfinished business. After watching the clip and feeling empowered, I still couldn't help but wonder how it would be to get under his sheets. My flesh was sending me selfish reminders that it hadn't been with a man in over seven years. I argued with my flesh, threw the word of God at it and even cursed it. However, the good that I would I did not that, but the evil which I shouldn't, that I did.

The next day I went against my right mind and decided to inbox him saying, I was ready to see him. He was excited and very soon after, he booked my flight. Once the confirmation email was delivered to me, I instantly thought what have I done? I knew it was wrong and disliked myself for the decision that I made, thinking what would be the consequences of this? I had about three weeks to think about my decision and the many ramifications. Who could I tell? What would I say? What would they think of me? Could it be any worse than what I already thought of myself?

I mustered the courage to tell three women who served differently in my life. The hardest of the three was my little sister. I remember coming down the stairs an emotional wreck. With tears still in my eyes, trembling in my voice and knots in my throat and stomach, I sat down on the couch across from her, looked her in her eyes and began giving her my disclosure. "I always want to be honest, and open with you, I'm not perfect, so I don't want you to put me on a pedestal nor think of me more profoundly than I am. I told her that I make mistakes and that I just recently made a big one that I already regretted." Pushing and breathing deeply past the huge knot in my throat I removed my perfect sister mask, and I told her that I had a trip planned to see a married man.

With shock in her eyes she looked at me for a minute, the next minute it was as if our roles were reversed, she pushed past her disappointment, and she gave me a sister's love and advice. She thought the solution was simple, she told me to cancel the trip and reimburse him the money. I couldn't have been more proud of her in that moment. She showed me how strong and brave she was, and she proved to me that she too loved me flaws and all. I exhaled because her confidence and trust in me never wavered after that day. She still respected me, and I continued to hold the title of her favorite big sister. For those reasons alone I vowed to be a woman that she could be proud of. I wanted to be her imperfectly perfect role model who did even what I said to do, so she could confidently do what I do.

I went back and forth with the idea of taking her advice to cancel the trip. I even told Houston many times that it wasn't a good idea, and he understood my feelings. I didn't want to be an adulterer. It was never my intention to break up a family or marriage. However, there was something about him that made making that decision hard for me. It wasn't about sex; it was about "What if?" A wise woman told me that it was important for me to make a decision that works for me. She challenged me to be clear of my expectations, put my big girl panties on and be willing to deal with whatever the consequences were to come. The more Houston and I would talk and the more that I learned about him over the weeks before my trip I began to conduct a mental systematic method for judging and comparing alternatives but no matter how many pros there were the one huge he's married con would always outweigh any good.

Three days before my trip the reality of things began to set in. I was often asked by him, and those who knew about the secret rendezvous "are you excited?" To which I would reply no, not excited. I wasn't enthusiastic or eager but rather, interested. My curiosity peaked because of "what if" but unlike the curious cat, I was trusting that it wouldn't kill me. I just needed to know what these feeling were. The best way I could describe it would be comparing it to a time where you're home alone, upstairs in your bed at night and as things are quiet, you hear a loud noise downstairs. Although you're afraid of the many dangerous possibilities you muster up enough strength and courage, get from out of your bed and begin to quietly tip toe your way down the stairs walking towards the sound of noise. Nothing about that experience is exciting but your curiosity to discover what it is and what if leads you to check things out so that your mind can be at ease.

Two days before leaving I awoke from my sleep in a panic again, thinking what have I done? How do I get out of this? One day before leaving talking to him that day calmed my anxiety, and I flirted with the idea of embracing him. 3:30 am the morning of my departure, I felt like a novice as I drove to the airport because this was the first time I've ever done anything like this, and that was once something that I was proud to say. I made it through the airport's checkpoint and comfortably sat at the gate as I awaited the time to board my flight.

While sitting, I heard a familiar voice behind me and I quickly looked back hoping that she didn't recognize me. At that moment I wanted to become invisible because I was afraid that my secret would be discovered if she asked me the common questions you ask someone you knowing that setting like; where are you going and who are you going to see? In about less than two minutes that voice became closer and closer as it was now in front of me with arms wide open and a smile on her face she hugged me. Of course, she asked me those same questions that I feared. I answered and to my relief, she didn't suspect anything but instead encouraged me to enjoy my trip. However, she wasn't alone when she walked away to grab a bite to eat her mother also asked me those dreaded questions to which I replied the same way "To Houston to visit my friend." With a smile on her face, a raised eyebrow and that motherly tone, she told me "be careful" at that moment I felt like a little girl so I smiled and agreed that I would be careful. It's funny what the old mothers know without us having to say a word. It reminded me of the time I fearfully told my mother I was no longer a virgin, and she replied that she already knew.

Shortly after we all boarded our flight and I was two destinations closer to him. After landing in Houston, I went into the restroom to freshen up, and I pulled my big girl panties up as the wise lady suggested. I made my way outside the airport and awaited his arrival. He greeted me with a smile and a quick but tight embrace then he placed my luggage in the car. On my seat lied twelve red roses. I was flattered by the attention and preparation he put into my arrival. As he drove he began to compliment me on my appearance; manicured hands and feet, form fitting sundress and my freshly laid hair. During the ride to the hotel, we laughed and talked as he laid out our plans for the weekend.

I checked into my hotel, and he carried my bags to my room. I know he had a wife but looking down at his finger it wasn't apparent because he removed his wedding band. Perhaps he didn't want any visual reminders of his obligation and commitment to his wife or maybe it was his way of living in his fantasy world. Whatever the reason I'm sure he couldn't ignore the observably deep indent that the ring made in his ring finger. Even though the sin was committed weeks ago in my heart opening the door to walk into my room with him somehow felt like the beginning of breaking all of the rules. I let him inside of my personal space, but it didn't feel comfortable, so I told him to get out and pushed him away.

At that moment so many thoughts and people invaded my mind. I thought about my little sister, and I remembered my convictions, morals, and standards but what was most surprising was when I thought about my perfect fit. It had been years since we were in touch but my love for that fit allowed me to know that anything with Houston would be accepting something less than perfect. I guess subconsciously he was the ruler that I measured others against. Looking at Houston and being with him didn't make me feel the way my perfect fit made me feel. I wasn't excited in his presence, and surprisingly my flesh didn't make its selfish request for satisfaction. I wasn't compelled to call my friend Nita so that she could talk me through this one. It was then when I realized that "What if?" was answered. I thought to myself "that was fast" it was less than two hours that I had been in Houston. Over $500 was spent but what I learned about myself in those hours and the days to come was priceless. The things and people that flashed through my mind when I was confronted with making a decision taught me so much about what matters to me the most.

My little sister – I vowed to be her imperfectly perfect role model. I knew she knew where I was and who I was with. I was confident that she would ask me questions about the weekend and I wanted to make sure that I was able to give her a good report. I wanted to be able to give her advice from a place that understood the temptations that she does and will experience even being a beautifully saved and single woman. To let her know that I can relate to the enticements of sin but yet not sin. I also wanted her to know that no matter how deep she may find herself falling in lust or temptation that with God's help it's never too late to grab hold of her convictions and morals to pull herself out of any messy situation.

My Perfect fit- Although we could never be, he captured and awakened my heart, mind, body, and soul. His love for me created a standard within me that I measure any potential mate against. I will not be satisfied or settle for anything less than that perfect fit.

Hours had passed after Houston left my room. He returned later to take me out for dinner. We caught up face to face as he was telling me things about him I never knew before some of which completely shocked me. As he shared his life, it became apparent to me he was right, coming there was just like visiting an old friend. He took me back to my hotel, hugged me and kissed me on the cheek as he expressed how happy he was to have seen me for the weekend. I agreed, and we went our separate ways. I stayed in Houston's city for a few days more. On Monday I checked out of my hotel, boarded my flight and as the doors of the airplane closed, and we took flight I closed the "What if?" chapter of my life.

6

TEACH ME HOW TO LOVE

The stories of Brianna and Brittany, Written by Brianna Triplett
and Brittany Capers

BRITTANY'S STORY

"Teach me how to love"- "Teach me how to love, teach me how to trust, teach me how to give even when I don't give enough/ teach me how to pray/tell me what to say/'cause I know without your love, I can't give love- so teach me Love."

At one time or another, this message has been the cry of almost every woman's heart when it comes to relational matters. Unfortunately, many women were once young girls who grew up without a positive, strong father or father-figure in their lives and lack the knowledge of how to truly <u>love</u>, <u>trust</u>, and <u>give</u> of themselves in a healthy manner in regards to their future romantic relationships as adults.

We have all heard of the countless stories of the "dead beat dad" or the dad who was there physically but not attentive emotionally in his daughter's upbringing. Most of us have heard of the common emotional, mental, relational, and in some cases physical and spiritual, effects and strains that those kinds of father-daughter relationships have had on the daughters. Although my experiences may be similar to many, the songs behind my stories are original. Dear Reader, please understand that you do not have to become a product of your physical environment or negative and unhealthy upbringing in anyway and that you are loved eternally, beyond any and every condition and situation by *Love* itself!

In February of 2013, after being single for a number of years- I began to feel very depressed and hopeless. 4 1/2 years prior, right after a relationship that was very meaningful to me at the time, ended- I vowed to never impatiently and ignorantly get into a meaningless relationship again and that I would be single while serving the Lord and others as a born-again Christian- until God led me to "the one" that would eventually become my husband. However, as time went by I began to question "Is there ANYONE out there that will truly love me for me?", "Does *true love* even exist?", and "Where are all of the good SINGLE, truly born-again, on fire, strong believing, handsome- Christian men?!"

Around Valentine's Day that year- I wrote these lyrics: <I love you with an everlasting love scripture> *"I AM LOVE"- (V1 :) I want to pour my heart out for you/I want to lavish you with affections from above/ I want you to soar on high with me/ I want to show you things that the human eye can't see/ So come with me//(hook:) And I will hold you in my arms forever/ And I will take you to a place where you will never be afraid/ We'll always be together/ From the beginning of time throughout forever/ / /(bridge:) I Am love and I never change/Forever and Always- I stay the same/ nothing can separate/This love I have for you will always remain/I Am love and I never change/Forever and Always-I stay the same/ nothing can separate/This love I have for you will always remain/ I Am Love/ I AM love/ God is Love!*

"Love" Himself clearly showed up and encouraged me through the writing of that song that *God is Love*! My heart was overwhelmed with joy in further realizing that this kind of love would love me unconditionally and would be with me throughout everything and all times. This message was further emphasized as I studied scriptures from the Holy Bible that confirmed it. I was reminded that God himself is the perfect example of love and what love is. I was also reminded of my Heavenly Father's great love for me (and the entire world) as the words of *(John 3:16)* seemed to jump off of the page and deep down into my heart and spirit: *"For God so loved the world that He gave His only begotten Son, that whosoever believeth in Him should not perish, but have everlasting life." "There is no greater love than to lay down one's life for one's friends."(John 15:13)*

They say that "love is an action word" and God (or *Love* himself) always acts out and shows us love through His very nature, character, and existence! He does not manufacture, imitate or perform *love*, it is simply who He is! Although my Heavenly Father's love was, is, and will always be perfect towards me- that's not the way I felt when I traveled back into time and researched (deeply searched again) the depths of my heart and mind of the love of my earthly father growing up and even into some of my adulthood; and it's definitely not the way that I felt when I thought of the flawed, imperfect, imitation love of any man towards me thus far!

Mentally throughout the years, I fell into many deep depressive, anxious, and post traumatic states (to simply and briefly put it) as a result of our constant back and forth, up and down, rollercoaster of events and emotions throughout my relationship with him. As I've done in some romantic relationships, I would notice the "red flags" from my dad earlier on as a warning to me that things weren't right- such as the way he would express his anger: physically, emotionally, and mentally to myself and others. However, I would ignore all of the signs and flags in an attempt to "sweep them under the rug" and to move forward in life. What I've learned since then about sweeping things under the rug is that the mess is still there! It's even spreading now underneath that rug. As we put that coffee table and other household items on top of it, it bears more weight and pressure. When you lift that rug up, that mess needs to be properly addressed and thrown away with the trash- forever! Trust me, there will be more dust and trash that will collect, giving us ample opportunities to do more sweeping- but we need to get rid of the mess as it comes instead of letting the pile build and just stay there!

Like sweeping trash under a rug, I overlooked those harmful and hurtful situations that would arise for years into my adulthood; and would even convince myself that because I didn't see it, it wasn't really there. It must have been dealt with right? Wrong! All of the hurtful pains of rejection, low self-esteem, abandonment, deceitfulness, unfaithfulness, mistrust, and lack of commitment and communication that were rooted and sprout up from itty- bitty little seedlings that my father planted into my heart and soul out of his own ignorance and lack of a healthy father-figure for himself; and through his words and actions- were all still there and more alive than ever!

All of those hurts carried on in some way or another in all of the relationships that I have had so far with men. With each relationship, by the grace of God- these symptoms were alleviated and greatly reduced, but some still remained. Even in my most recent relationship from the end of last year, I felt as if I couldn't trust my then boyfriend towards the end of our relationship. I began to call him so often and frequently in an attempt to "check up on him" because I thought that he would have less of a chance of cheating on me if I did. Although I thought that relationship was headed toward marriage, in the relationship that I had years before that I also thought was leading to marriage- I thought to myself "surely when we are married, he will cheat on me and leave me. We will end up having a divorce." I thought like that halfway through most of my relationships because that is what was modeled before me.

Although I was a born-again Christian, who was educated and tried to encourage and minister to others in different areas- I secretly felt as if whatever marriage I got into, if I ever got married- would not have the ability to last; that my husband wouldn't have the capacity to love me deeply because I was not that special or lovable to begin with. Through time, I've realized that I've let some really good guys who are now happily married go (before they got married) because I didn't know how to trust them. In turn, they didn't know how to fully love or give their love to me based on my lack of trust for them. I also realized that I let some rotten ones go- and thank God for that! You know, the ones that come along and act like they are your "Boaz" or your "Isaacs", when they really are your "Ishmaels?"

Even though my father wasn't always there for me and I've rejected some and have been rejected in relationships - I truly thank God for never leaving or forsaking me as His daughter or any of His children for that matter! In the summer of 2012, as I reflected on the deep abandonment and rejection that I felt from my earthly father and past relationships at the time- I jotted these words down in my journal and began to sing them out loud. *(Psalm 27:10) "Though my father and mother forsake me, the LORD will receive me."* *"Never Leave Me"-* *(V1:) You stick closer than my brother/ More nurturing than my mother/ You're more loyal than my sistahs/ Protect me better than my father// (hook:) "I will never leave you, nor forsake you"- that's what You said!/ You keep all of Your promises- In You I can depend/ To never leave me, never leave me- No!/ You won't ever leave me, nor forsake me, nor forsake me!"* The book of Deuteronomy also brings emphasizes to this message *in (Deuteronomy 31:6) "Be strong and courageous. Do not be afraid or terrified because of them, for the LORD your God goes with you; he will never leave you nor forsake you."*

All of the experiences that I've had from my relationship with my father from childhood through this time in adulthood have been reflected in some kind of way in romantic relationships that I have had throughout the years as well. At this point, I choose to deal with the issues as I learn to *heal* from them. They have held me back for too long and I now know that a large part of my singleness was due to the need of healing in many areas. The late Pastor, Best-Selling Author, and Motivational Speaker Dr. Myles Munroe paraphrased in his book *"Single, Married, Separated and Life after Divorce"* that God will not put two halves of two different people together in order to make one whole, complete person; but that He instead desires to put two, whole people together so that they can complement and add on to each other!

While recognizing that I am fully incapable of being perfect, I recognize that I serve a God who is fully capable of perfection and that He is the love and "the one" that I've been looking for all along! Through Him, I am free to love and trust. He is the one that truly teaches me how to love! His character of unconditional love, protection, trustworthiness, faithfulness, attentiveness, strength, humbleness, honesty, and sincerity is the highest standard of what I should consider when I consider *love*. On Valentine's Day, during a different year than "I AM LOVE" was written- I recorded these lyrics on the voice recorder of my cell phone (at the time): "Free in You"- (V1 :) It took some time for me to truly find "the one" for me/ but now I've finally come to realize that You are all I need/ You took ahold of my pain, shame, faults, flaws, and insecurities/and You erased all the hurt inside/destroyed my pride/and restored me- now I am free//(hook:) I'm free to love/free to trust/free to live my life for You/I'm free to dance/I'm free to lift my hands/I'm free to live my life brand new in You- I'm free in You!//

Since I've vowed to be single until God sent me "the one", I was in another relationship that didn't last. This breakup sent me through a series of deep depression. I was at an age and time in my life where I thought "this has to be him... "The one." "This one is gonna last forever." When it didn't turn out that way, I questioned God and asked "Lord, what is going on here? I thought I was your daughter! I thought I was serving you! I thought I loved you and you loved me! Where is my 'Boaz' Lord? Where is my Godly husband that I can call my earthly King? Where is he?...WHERE IS HE?!"

As a result of that breakup- after deep depression set in, and after spending time in the word and in prayer I journaled and recorded the lyrics to *"Greater than any Man"*- *(V1 :) Only You can satisfy/ this dry thirst that's deep inside/ and this hunger I can't deny/ I've searched for alternatives- thought it would be much easier/ 'till I found out it only got worse// (Bridge:) No one, nowhere, nothing can bring- satisfaction like You can/ Oh, Lord You make my heart sing- greater than any man/ in You I Am complete/ and I lack no good thing/ Oh Lord, You make my heart sing- greater than any man// (Hook:) Oh, Your love is so much stronger than (any man)/ Your love is so much deeper than (any man)/ Your love is more desired than (any man)/ Your love is so much greater than- any man!//*

Would Have Been Nice
Brianna Triplett (2007)

I never needed you to be there when I was born,
Or hear my first word,
Or see my first step,
Or teach me how to ride a bicycle,
Or to hang my drawings on the refrigerator,
Or listen to my poetry.

I never needed you to give me advice about what to wear,
Or the importance of school,
Or to tell me what the super bowl is,
Or keep me up to date with the latest video games.
I never needed you to tell me how to get a man,

Treat a man,
Teach me how to love a man,
Keep a man,
You understand?

I never needed you to cheer me on at my high school graduation,
Or college graduation,
Or scare any knuckle head guys I dated,
Or tell me I was pretty or smart,
Or special or worthy,
Of anybody's attention,
Or love,
Or tell me how to keep my legs shut,
Or show me how a man is supposed to take care of his family,
Or hold down a job,
Or be the king of his household,
Or take care of me.

I'm grown now, and independent no thanks to you,
So I can take care of myself!
I never needed you! I never will need you!
But maybe….ever once in a while,
I sit down,
And I think to myself,
"Would have been nice"

BRIANNA'S STORY

He smiled at me, mouth full of diamonds, bright eyes like stars, as he told me how beautiful I was. I smiled hesitantly and looked down at the floor; something about the way he said it made me believe that maybe this time it had to be true. At 24 years of age, this was my first time meeting him, but looking at his broad nose, and confident smile, I felt like I had seen him somewhere before. "I want you to know something" he said, "I am not going to let anybody hurt you! If someone ever tried to hurt you they would have to put me away for life! Let me know if you ever need anything because I am here to provide for you." I nodded as he studied me, noticing that his words were slowly softening my calloused heart he said, "I am the earthly representation of God's love for you. God could not have put a better man in your life to fill this role." I thought about the men that filled that role prior to him, and was hoping that he was right, "Do you believe me? Do you believe that I am going to take good care of you?" I nodded a nod that was nervous and excited all at the same time, then he said, "I just want you to know that you can trust me."

1 Year 5 Months Later

He looks at me with intense anger and my eyes well up with utter disbelief. I've seen this look before, it's all too familiar, and I know what's about to happen next, and then finally the 1st hit comes. I am too shocked to feel where it lands or with what intensity it landed, but I saw it coming. I frantically run up the stairs, heart beating wildly, hands grasping for the walls as I climb the steps with my hands and feet, trying to find stability in a world that just turned upside down. I did not know where I was going, but I knew that I had to get away, all of a sudden it feels like handfuls of follicles are being ripped out of my head as I start to involuntarily descend I realize I am being dragged by my hair down the stairs. Once my journey is complete he turns me around so that I can see the sick mixture of disgust and amusement on his face, as he pushes me into the wall and the door and ultimately pushes me into my sisters bedroom and unto her bed like a football player pushing a blocking sled, "Oh God, not this again", I think, as I cross my legs and shake my head back and forth traveling back to the back of a car at age 18, when a 23 year old man I thought would never cause me harm, betrayed me, stealing my innocence and my trust. He say's something, but although I see his mouth moving all I hear is my heart beat, and my deep breaths, as my ears mute words that could have hurt worse than his hands. He walks away and I breathe a quick sigh of relief before calling the police. His punishment: 1 night in jail, and a 2 year order of protection. My relationship with my Dad has not been the same since.

How to Build a Wall

You see, up until the age of 24 I believed that another man was my father, and my mother and this man got a divorce when I was a young child. For years I witnessed the abuse my mother endured in her various relationships, it was so bad that we secretly fled to another state for a year to avoid one of her abusers. I always told myself that I would never allow a man to lay his hands on me. When I became an adult I received a Master's Degree in Psychology and became a human service worker for a season at a domestic violence shelter to help other women gain a sense of control over their lives again. In my own attempts to show a man that he did not have the authority to bring me physical harm, sometimes I would act defensive when there was never a need to, but I needed them to know that I could fight back if need be right? I mean, all men lay their hands on women and it was just a matter of when, where, why and how right? Wrong. One of the meanings of my name is, Strong. I made sure to live up to the meaning of my name, even if it meant pointing out my partners weaknesses, or making them feel inferior or intimidating them, so that somehow I could prove to them how strong I was.

Looking for affection in all the wrong places, looking for love in all the wrong faces….

Eventually after the man that I thought was my father moved on with his life, I felt forgotten, and abandoned, until I grew up and graduated high school with a full scholarship to attend college. "That's my daughter", he would proudly say, "She is so smart, she got that from me." Sticking out his chest, he would strut around after Church and at family functions and show his daughter off like some trophy or other prized possession. When someone I confided in slipped up and told him I lost my full scholarship I knew I wouldn't be hearing from him anytime soon and I didn't. I felt rejected. What did I have to do to get his attention? What do I have to do to get anybody's attention? I craved attention, especially attention from a man. Attention seemed to make up for all the years I didn't have a father to tell me I looked pretty, at dance recitals, at graduation, at prom, on my 1st date, and it was always a bonus when a man twice my age gave my attention, but when the wrong man knows that you are a woman that likes attention, he will do anything to find out just how far you are willing to go to get his attention and keep his attention, and after you have lost his attention, he moves on, leaving you wanting more.

"Daddy Issues"

So when I met this man at the age of 24 years old, 1 day after my 24th birthday at a New Year's Service at my Church and he told me that he was my Dad, which was later confirmed with a DNA test, and he told me how beautiful and loved I was, I wanted to believe him. Within the 1st year of knowing him I saw the signs of abuse but tried to ignore them.

I was never allowed to speak my opinions about life, about society about God without being called disrespectful or confrontational when I disagreed with his way of thinking.

My Dad would yell at me or speak to me in a condescending tone and then say, "I'm sorry, BUT if you hadn't …" and when I could not seem to get over whatever disagreement had just taken place as quickly as he would have liked I was just "too sensitive."

He would not let me comfortably start calling him "Dad" on my own when I first met him, and wanted me to address him as such at all times, even though I had just met him in my adult life, and did not feel comfortable using that terminology yet.

He found every opportunity he could to tell me how I was not like his oldest daughter, my sister Brittany, and how I should be more like her, instead of the woman I had already become.

He criticized the way that I dressed, every relationship I entered into, how I handled my finances, and even how I spent my free time.

Our very first argument was him criticizing the way I drove, MY vehicle, and yelling at me, and forcing me into the passenger seat and making me ride in the passenger seat of MY vehicle every time we went anywhere together after that. Just like I lost the ability to control my own steering wheel, I lost any control that I had over my own personal life, and I was allowing my Dad to lead me, when I should have given the wheel to God, and allowed him to direct me. When I came into my father's life I was a fully raised, educated, employed, and even engaged young woman, but he felt the need to break me down, and raise me all over again in his attempt to make up for lost time. The woman I had become was not one that he was proud of and he wanted to mold me and shape me into his image. Before I knew it I had called off the wedding ceremony which was already mostly planned and ended my engagement with my fiancé. I moved in with my Dad and after paying a security deposit for an apartment to move out once I realized the manipulation and abuse that was taking place, was somehow convinced to get a refund on a nonrefundable security deposit that I paid and to continue to live with him so he could as he said, "prove to you that I can be a good father." I felt like I could not go to certain movies, or watch certain television shows, or go to concerts, or comedy shows because he was constantly questioning my spirituality. He met me for the first time at a Church and on that I day I told him that I was saved, but he constantly made me question my salvation, and would try to convince my siblings who I had an amazing relationship with, to question my salvation as well. When I told him I wanted to get involved in ministry, he would tell me that I was not ready. When I told him that I wanted to get into a relationship, he told me, that I was still not where I needed to be. According to him I was never good enough, for the good things that I knew God had in store for me.

Not Ready For Love

When hanging out and chatting with potential mates I would often come down on myself and where I was at financially, educationally, spiritually and emotionally, even physically because of what my Dad had convinced me of concerning myself. My lack of self-esteem was unattractive and the hatred that I felt for myself was obvious. No man wants to attach himself to a woman that does not know how to love herself. How does a woman that doesn't know how to love herself, expect a man to love her, or expect a man to feel confident that she knows how to love him. Eventually men got tired of trying to convince me that I was loveable and moved on to women who were already aware of their worth as a woman and were ready to love and be loved without needing constant affirmation from men because it was given to them by God.

When that dark day came 1 year and 5 months after meeting my father it should not have surprised me. After that incident my trust issues ran deep like an ocean. When the next man came into my life that told me he loved me, and wanted to protect me, and provide for me, I was wondering what truth was behind his words, behind his mouth full of diamonds and bright eyes like stars and I was determined not to believe him until further investigation proved his innocence. I was constantly questioning potential mates until they just could not take it anymore, like psychologists they would quickly diagnose me, "You know what your problem is? You have trust issues"; "You know what? You have self-esteem issues" and each one quickly ran out of my life. "Maybe my Dad is right" I thought to myself. "I'm not ready for a relationship."

The 1st man I believed was my father, taught me that I had to work for a man's attention, and honey I worked, in how I dressed, in what I said, and the goals I tried to accomplish in life, and I opened the door that made it easier for men to take advantage of me as soon as they recognized how hungry I was for affection and attention.

The men that came in and out of my mother's life trying to play "house" and be a father figure to me taught me how to be strong, and never let a man lay his hands on me, but my hard exterior only ran the good ones away and made the wrong ones want to tear me down. I was so busy building a defense around myself in relationships that I was not taking the time to build up my man, and men need to feel secure in their leadership position in your life and not feel like they are in a constant battle to be the king of your heart after God.

The second man I came to know as "Dad", taught me what it felt like to be loved, and called beautiful and to finally feel safe, to be provided for, to let my hard exterior fall to the wayside, only to violently rip that sprouting trust away like a flower rising out of the ground being plucked, with emotional and physical abuse. I bitterly had to rebuild the wall I allowed to crumble brick by brick, the wall that had protected me, yet hindered me, so in actuality it harmed me, for years.

My Dad taught me how to never trust a man, period. I had become one of those mad black women I heard comedians joke about in movies, with "daddy issues." I was convinced that all of these self-professing saviors were just Satan in disguise, deep down I knew that it was not true, but I could not stop believing it. I had been conditioned for so many years to believe that my Dad was the earthly representation of my heavenly father that I even began to question God.

Father to the Fatherless

But let me tell you a about a father, whose ways will make you love him first, love and appreciate yourself because you are his, and love others as a result. My mother committed suicide and my Dad and I had a difficult relationship, but I hold on to *(Psalm 27:10 NLT)* *"Even if my father and mother abandon me, the Lord will hold me close."* My Dad tried to convince me that if I was not close to my earthly father that, that was an indicator that I could never truly be close to my heavenly father, but in fact, the hard times that I faced with my earthly Dad just continued to reveal to me on a deeper level how awesome my heavenly father was, is, and will always be. God said in *(Jeremiah 31:3 NIV)* *"I have loved you with an everlasting love; I have drawn you with UNFAILING kindness."* God's love never pushes us away, never runs away, never runs out, but it draws us to him, it is constantly overflowing, it is a love that does not give up, but is persistent, and consistent. *(1John 4:8 NIV)* actually *says "....God is love..."* and *(1Corinthians 13:8)* lets us know that *"Love never fails"*, if God is love, and love never fails, God never fails.

Do you need peace? God will never fail you. Do you need joy? God will never fail you. Do you need deliverance? God will never fail you. Do you need healing? God will never fail you. Looking for a protector? God will never fail you. Looking for a provider? God will never fail you. God will never fail you! God will never fail you! Because God is love and love NEVER fails.

Once you begin to love whose you are, you finally can love who you are. Woman you are a "good thing" (*Proverbs 18:22*) you are "*fearfully and wonderfully made*" (*Psalm 139:14*), you are "*worth far more than rubies*" (*Proverbs 31:10*) God "*has searched you, and he knows you*" and yet he loves you. (*Psalm 139:1*) He "*delights in you and rejoices over you with singing*" (*Zephaniah 3:17*) God has placed you "*above and not beneath*" (*Deuteronomy 28:13*), you are royalty (*1 Peter 2:9*) and you are loved by the King of Kings and Lord of Lords. If you have God, you have love, and you can love, because God is love. You can love yourself, your family, your friends, your coworkers, your enemies, complete strangers, and eventually you can love a man, but it all begins with opening your heart to God.

After my self-made idol, (my Dad) fell far from the comfortable cushion of his throne, I've cried out to the one who never left my side, and this is what he taught me about love in words and in deeds, "*Love is patient, love is kind, it does not envy, it does not boast, it is not proud. It does not dishonor others, it is not self-seeking, it is not easily angered, it keeps no record of wrongs, and love does not delight in evil but rejoices with the truth. It always protects, always trust, always hopes always perseveres.*" (*1 Corinthians 13:4-7*)

God's love is sacrificial, demonstrated in the death Jesus died daily in his everyday life so that others could know him, and in the ultimate death that he died on the cross for the atonement of our sins, and in his resurrection on the 3rd day so that we could have everlasting life and one day rise with him as well. God's love is unconditional; he loves you in spite of who you are, where you are, who you were, where you were, what you did, when you did it, why you did it, how you did it, and where you did it. He has seen you in your most natural state, flaws and all, the "you" that makeup can't conceal, that extensions cannot accentuate and he absolutely loves you.

(*Psalm 17:8* NIV) tells you that you are the apple of his eye. When we fall in love with God, a love that will be our first true romance everything else in life will begin to fall in place.

Some may wonder why I would go to this extent, telling such personal details concerning my father and myself. The bible clearly states in (*John 8:32* NIV) *"...The truth will set you free."* (*Galatians 5:1* NIV) says *"It is for freedom that Christ has set us free."* I want to be free to have joy, to experience peace, and to love freely, like Christ freely loves us (*1 John 4:10* NIV) The enemy wants you to keep the test that you have been through a secret, because he wants everyone around you to fail that test when their time comes, but your test is a part of your testimony, and there is healing in releasing it, not just for others, but for yourself. I cannot begin to tell you the number of women that I have been able to minister to, by sharing what I have been through. What is done in the dark, has to come to the light, it's imperative that we don't hold on to baggage, because it will weigh us down in the long run, for me, it was time to let go so that I can go forward. Everyone has a story to tell. I also realize after having worked in the human service field for years, that many people have experienced emotional, and physical abuse in their childhood and even their adulthood from their parents or guardians that they did not recognize as abuse and I would like to raise awareness about a sensitive subject, especially in the African American community where "what's done at home, stays at home." That mentality is crippling our community, and holding us hostage to our past trauma. I am currently seeking spiritual and professional guidance, and so is my father, and we are in a season of restoration and I am not sure how long it will take, but because I have forgiven him, and we are both seeking help I know that it will not be long until we have a healthy and loving father daughter relationship with one another, and guess what? That makes me appreciate how good God is all the more, how he can take a situation that the enemy meant for evil and use it for his good, by causing my Dad to seek him all the more for healing from the hurts of his past that he has not dealt with that has hindered from being all God has called him to be, and for helping me to recognize how deeply I needed to turn to God for the love that I needed from him and him alone, so that I could freely give that love to myself, and to others and not continue to search for what I would never find in a man. So many women jump into relationships hoping that a man, will give them joy, and give them peace, and fill every void, but only God can make us whole, we can't put pressure on a mortal to do what only the immortal one can do and because I had not received the love that I was hoping I would from father figures, and my actual biological father, it had suddenly become the responsibility of the men that I was dating to provide that love, I wanted love for all the wrong reasons, but my heavenly father taught me that love is not about receiving but about giving and I am now ready to love, because love comes from God, and everyone who loves has been born of God and knows God, if we love one another God lives in us and His love is made complete in us. (*1 John 4:7-12* NIV)

If you did not have an earthly father to teach you how to love, please do not fret; allow your heavenly father, the definer, and definition of love, to teach you how to love.

7

BEAUTY & THE BEAST

Like the Disney classic, "Beauty and the Beast" I was once a vibrant, healthy and beautiful daughter of The King. One day when I was a young girl, Satan came knocking at my door. Knowing whose daughter I was, he tempted me with some of his guilty pleasures to which I proudly declined but little did I know that from that moment on his anger was kindled against me and his mission to steal, kill and destroy in my life began. Slowly but steadily my ugly beast of life's circumstances turned me into something even I couldn't stand to see. Every experience left a horrendous scar, and Satan made sure to leave me with a magnifying mirror so I could always be reminded of how hideous my flaws made me. He told me often that I was unlovable and not valuable. Each time his words cut deep like a knife. I was so sedated that I had no memory of who I was. I forgot that I was The Kings Daughter; I forgot that I was made in my father's image and after His likeness. I forgot that even though I was imperfect God included my sins to the nailed cross.

I'm fat, and I sometimes feel ugly. My teeth are too small, yellow and chipped. My skin is too pale. My thighs rub together when I walk. My breast sag. My stomach is too big. My butt has cellulite, it's not firm or big enough. My face is too full, I only have one dimple. My lips are pink with markings of brown. My smile isn't picture perfect. The birthmark on my forehead looks like Africa. I'm short and my legs are hairy. When I'm furious I curse, I've cursed at my son. Sometimes I'm jealous and possessive, I can be stubborn and I often think I'm right. I'm a perfectionist. I'm too emotional. I love too hard. I over think way too much. I'm not good with finances, I've robbed you in tithes and offering. I'm an introvert and often prefer to be alone or in small groups. I've lied and have been lied on. I've cheated and have been cheated on. I hit a woman. I've kissed a girl. I've been arrested and thrown in jail. I've been sexually abused and emotionally ill-treated. I've stolen. I've gossiped. I've been drunk and I've inhaled marijuana. I've fornicated countless times, I've masturbated, I've watched pornography, I've had a son out of wedlock and I've kissed a married man. I've been judgmental and self-righteous. I've carried un-forgiveness in my heart. I've been manipulative. I've procrastinated. I've been depressed and I've contemplated suicide. I've broken laws. I've been passive and I've been too aggressive. I've been haughty and I've been prideful. I've been hypocritical. I've questioned if you were real. I've thought about walking away from my son and I've thought about walking away from you.

But I didn't have to tell you all of that because you told me *(Jeremiah 1:5) "Before I formed thee in the belly, I knew thee, and before thou came forth out of the womb I sanctified thee, and ordained thee a prophet unto the nations."* You know that I'm imperfect and weak. My flaws are deep like fresh cut scars, but yet you still consider me flawless, having no defects or faults that could diminish my value. Like Moses, I keep asking you "Who am I" that I should aid your people in their deliverance? Don't you remember this thorn in my flesh that I've repeatedly asked you to remove? Instead, you reply *(2 Corinthians 12:9) "My grace is sufficient for thee; for my strength is made perfect in weakness."* I tell you that I'm not eloquent, but you say "who hath made man's mouth…? Have not I thee the Lord? Now therefore go, and I will be with thy mouth, and teach thee what thou shalt say. *(Exodus 4:11)* *"I tell you that I'm fearful, but you reply: (2 Timothy 1:7) "For I have not given you the spirit of fear; but of power, and of love, and of a sound mind."* I tried to hide my nakedness from your presence, but you called unto me the same way you did Adam saying "Courtney Where art thou?" Then I said to you they will not believe me, nor hearken unto my voice because of my sins, but you say to me *(Jeremiah 1:8)* *"Be not afraid of their faces; for I am with thee to deliver thee."*

Lastly, I say but Father, How can I minister your Perfect Word, and I'm an imperfect vessel? You calmly replied, *(1 Peter 4:11)* *"If any man speak as the oracles of God; if any man minister, let him do it as of the ability which I giveth; that I in all things may be glorified through Jesus Christ, to whom be praise and dominion for ever and ever amen. Beloved daughter, think it not strange concerning the fiery trial which is to try you as though some strange thing happened to you. But rejoice in as much as you are a partaker of Christ's suffering: that when His glory shall be revealed, ye may be glad also with exceeding joy."*

Then you asked me, "Now will you say yes to my will and yes to my way?" You told me that I had to decide whether or not I wanted to solely impress people or influence them to change. Impressing deals with the mind and feelings. Influence is the process of producing effects. It's the difference between getting someone to think that they should change and have the effect on someone that causes them to change. You told me that I could impress people from a distance with my titles, by the clothes I wear and the expressive way I communicate. However, to influence someone, I must remove my mask and allow them to get close enough to me. When they do, they'll be able to see all of the flaws and scars I try to hide, but you promised me that it would be ok because a quality of leadership isn't perfection but instead credibility. People must be willing and able to trust me, or they will not follow me. With a moment to think, I chose yes, and decided to trust you. I promised to build credibility by being transparent about my imperfections believing that your name will be glorified in the end.

For so long I was too afraid and embarrassed by my shameful scars because it reminded me of my wounding past. Afraid of scrutiny I made a concerted effort to keep my immoral acts from being made public. However, you wanted me to do just the contrary. You wanted me to expose myself so that others who witnessed my trials and tribulations would also know of your healing power in my life. You wanted me to share my story so that others would be freed to tell theirs.

You promised me that you would never leave me exposed without covering me the same way you did for Adam and Eve when they were naked, and you clothed them with coats of skin. You told me that you covered the real me in the natural, and you'll do the same in the spiritual. You explained that in the natural the real me is on the inside, covered with your blood the same way that spiritually my sins are covered by your blood and that you created a beautiful and durable exterior to protect me, and that's what the people see.

I began to think about all of the injuries both big and small that can happen to the body internally and externally that can result in a scar. I remembered when I visited my cousin's son in the hospital as a premature baby. Upon my visit, I noticed that his stomach was outside of his body and how the doctors covered it with bandages. They did it because if they hadn't the particles from an unclean environment would cause an infection that would create more damage that could further threaten and delay his healing process. Over time his bandages came off, his stomach healed properly, and we now bear witness to his healing. But before the doctors could remove the bandage and expose his belly they had to make sure that a certain level of healing had taken place and that he was strong enough to fight off any possible infections that could arise.

If you had a physical injury and it turned into an infection, would you put a Band-Aid on the wound to fix the problem? NO! You would have to take the bandage off; cleanse it so that it can properly heal. When we experience internal wounds such as a broken heart, rape, divorce or loss of a loved one it is important to remember that God cares for us, covers us, protects us, cleanses us, and he heals us. God will not expose us to an unclean environment before we are strong enough to fight. If he exposes us, it's either because we're healed, or another level of healing needs to take place.

When caring for my physical injuries the first thing that I usually do is cleanse it from germs so that it can heal properly. Pouring alcohol onto an open wound isn't pleasant and often stings, but I know that it's working for my good the same way God uses my intentional trials and tribulations and works them for my good because I love Him and because I'm called according to His purpose. When dealing with my emotional wounds I realized that carrying around feelings of guilt, shame and fear made the healing process much more problematic. Getting myself to the place where I knew that where I am and who I am today, right now, in my life is good enough for God's love, forgiveness and acceptance were one of the foundations to receiving my inner healing. Knowing that God wasn't angry or disappointed in me created an atmosphere where I could freely turn my burdens and cares over to Him because I know He cares for me. I realized that carrying around the baggage of shame was weighing me down and ultimately hindering my inner healing and peace because it mentally separated me from His healing work in my life. I had to believe that God was not angry with me, I am forgiven, and my sins were washed away by the blood of Christ. Each time I refused His forgiveness, it was if I was nailing Him back to the cross.

My scars signify that some damage to my body has occurred. They aren't attractive and often embarrassing but on the other hand, my scars indicate that I've healed from those experience and if my blemishes weren't restored I wouldn't be able to say that I don't look like what I've been through. The mere fact that I have a scar shows that I was in a fight and that those things that were trying to kill me may have hurt me or bruised me, but ultimately I rose again and got the victory. I could've chosen to continually cover up my scar with makeup pretending that it's not there but once the makeup comes off I have to deal with the fact that the scar is still there. Instead of feeling like my scars were marks of the beast himself I chose to embrace my scars as perfect beauty marks that reflect my strength and healing as a victorious overcomer.

After your crucifixion and resurrection, you came to your disciples appearing in the room where they had locked themselves in for safety and stood in their midst saying "Peace be unto you." You showed them your hands and your side where they nailed and pierced you and when they saw you they were glad. But Thomas, one of your disciples was not with them when you came. The others told him that they saw you but Thomas said *(John 20:25) "Except I shall see in his hands the print of the nails, and put my finger into the print of the nails, and thrust my hand into his side, I will not believe."* So eight days later you reappeared to your disciples including Thomas and stood in their midst saying *"Peace be unto you."* You said to Thomas *"Reach hither thy hand and thrust it into my side, and be not faithless but believing."* Then Thomas answered and said unto you *"My Lord and My God"* You replied, *(John 20:29) "Thomas because thou have seen me, thou have believed; blessed are they that have not seen, and yet have believed."*

You knew that there would be some Thomas's that would question my credibility until they were able to see my scars. You also heard the cries of your people in their times of despair and anguish. Those that felt alone in their struggles, those who believed that there was no hope of deliverance and healing for them. They told you that unless they were able to see someone else with the same struggles delivered and healed they wouldn't believe. So as you did with Thomas, you appeared in their life at a time when they had locked themselves away from the world out of fear. You stood in their midst and said: "Peace be unto you." You allowed them to see the scars of one of your beloved children and said to them "Be not faithless but believe."

I knew you healed me when they picked at the "she kissed a girl" wound, and it didn't hurt, when they thrust their fingers through the "she killed a woman" scar, and it didn't bleed. When they gossiped and tried to defame my character and I no longer questioned myself. When he tried to get me to argue, and I didn't become angry but walked away. Healing was when I was able to look at my scar, remember the story of the painful experience but no longer felt the pain.

Flawed but Flawless

How could you think that my flaws were beautiful? How could you consider me a virtuous woman with a price that's far beyond rubies? How is it that in your eyes I shine bright like a diamond?

All diamonds are assigned value based on their cut, color, clarity, and carat weight. Cut refers to the way a diamond cutter or jeweler cuts a raw diamond to give it a shape that allows light to bounce from one sheer line to another, retracting light and causing the diamond to sparkle intensely when the sun hits it. Diamonds can range from no color to white, pink, blue, yellow and champagne. Clarity measures the amount of imperfections present in a diamond and carat is the portion of the weight or size of the diamond. These factors determine the rarity and therefore the cost of the diamond. The rarer a diamond is the more expensive it will cost to own.

Inclusions, flaws or blemishes can be used as proof of a diamond's natural origin. So the mere fact that I have faults, scars, sins, imperfections, that weigh too much, all prove that I belong to you and because of my rarity the only way that I could be purchased was for you to lie down your life for me.

The Gemological Institute of America states that in 1952, Richard T Liddicoat, along with Marquis Person, Joe Phillips, Robert Crowning Sheild and Bert Krashes began to work on a new diamond grading system which they named the diamond grading and evaluation appraisal. They made new assessments to the make, color, and clarity of the diamond. The three changes that were completed during the 1970s were first; the internally flawless grade was added. GIA noticed that many diamonds were being aggressively cut to remove any surface blemishes and thereby reducing the quality "makeup" of the diamonds. The internally flawless grade gave diamond manufacturers a choice to leave blemishes on the surface of the stone, and receive a grade higher than VVS; the second change was made in response to a growing number of diamonds of very low quality being cut. The last change to the clarity grading system took place in the 90s when the term "imperfect" was changed to "included."

Oh Lord, I am the clay, you are the potter, and I'm the work of your hand. I was marred, so you made me over and shaped me as it pleased you. You called me light and instructed me to shine before men that they may see your good works, and glorify you.

You knew that I was flawed and corrupted by sin, but yet you didn't treat me as my sins deserved. You showed mercy and changed the grading system forever by becoming the ultimate sacrifice for me. Now I'm saved by grace through faith. The beautiful part is you're not a respecter of persons. The blood you shed on the cross included the sins and flaws of an imperfect me, she and him.

All of a sudden the answer to my questions became obvious when I read somewhere "She's a woman of substance a beauty and a beast. Only a king can appreciate that." All of this time I thought it was Satan, the beast himself cutting me with his claws, but yet it was you perfecting me and molding me into a beautiful flawless diamond.

Natural Beauty
Dawn Flakes

L'OREAL, Maybelline, and Cover-girl could have done nothing to mask my imperfections, scars, and flaws; neither could the best put together first aid kit with all its ace bandages, Band-Aids and gauze. See my battle scars went way beyond superficial they dove into the deepest innermost parts of my soul. I'm telling you I don't look like what I've been through and had it not been for grace and new mercies daily my story would not have been told. You see the makeup artist I had become over the years or should I say over the tears was not by choice but came out of necessity. I would never have thought years down the line that the truth foundation of my creation would bring out the best in me. My expertise and knowledge of application manifested through each and every circumstance my life had dealt. Molestation, rape and a crash survivor and due to it all hurt, shame and pain were all I felt. How dare guilt hold me captive to the point that forgiveness was possible for others but not for me! I believe someone owes this track star a gold medal because I ran so fast for so long from what was destined to be. I guess the most intriguing yet baffling question is, how is it that after all, I have been through God…YES GOD still has a use for me? He's the great revealer behind my concealer. The one who counted me worthy, He spoke to my insecurities and calmed my storm raging inside. He began removing my lipstick and my eye shadow and showed me I had no reason to hide. I began to see what HE spoke, and I began to be what HE said. I began to walk in my calling, by the Father, Son, and Spirit I am led. So here I stand today unbound and unchained because whom the Son sets free is free indeed. Today I bless HIM for every hill and every mountain and for the blood of the Lamb that was shed for me. To the young ladies, God will place in my path, you are the true benefactors of my testimony. I have been tested and tried in the fire that I may do for you what I could not do for me, and that is to uncover the cover-up and help heal whatever wound there may be. To let you, YES YOU know that you were worth dying for in all your Natural Beauty.

8

BEAUTY FOR ASHES

Life after Death

In May of 2010, not even two months after the accident to my surprise I discovered that I was pregnant. I often heard that for every death there's a baby born, but this was too soon. Mixed with emotions, ultimately happy, how could I selfishly be excited about life growing inside of me when I was the cause of someone else's life taken away? Dazed with hurt, guilt, and fear I thought how did this happen? Who can I tell? I was like the walking dead and yet there was something on the inside of me that felt so alive. This was the pregnancy I've anticipated and longed for all of my life, and finally, it was here. However, I couldn't help but to feel like it came at the worse and most inconvenient time. Unemployed, how could I financially support this gift from God? Not only that but I was still under investigation from the fatal accident and possibly facing jail time. I've heard stories of women giving birth in prison, and I began to think this would also be the case for me. Perhaps this was my punishment and ultimately what I deserved. Mentally, physically and spiritually it seemed that I was too weak and incapable of carrying this life full term. I was convinced that the stress alone would cause me to miscarry. There were days that I couldn't eat or sleep. My only nourishment came from the word of God that I had stored up on the inside of me like a bear during hibernation, but yet I gained forty pounds, putting me at the heaviest I've been my entire life. Knowing that no two pregnancies are the same I knew that this was not going to be like any pregnancy or birth that I have delivered before. There was no possible way to abort this one and a surrogate mother wasn't an option. It was mine for the keeping and up to me to deliver.

On July 1, 2010, a few months after conception I had given birth, and the name was "Purpose." Since I was a little girl, I often wondered and guessed what it was that God would birth through me. I envisioned being Dr. Hawkins an obstetrician naturally helping women through their labor and delivery process but God had other plans. One early morning while I was cleaning the bathrooms at my part time position with Abundant Care CCS, God began to speak to me while I was cleaning. He showed me how physicians used gloves to protect their hands while they are performing surgery. Then He took me to *(Mark 16:18) "They shall lay hands on the sick, and they shall recover."* That's when He whispered every so softly in my ear and called me "Dr. Courtney" and explained that my purpose is to spiritually coach and assist the broken through their delivery and healing process. My mission is to: *"Proclaim good news to the poor and bind up the brokenhearted. To proclaim freedom for the captive and release from darkness for the prisoners. To proclaim the year of the LORD's favor and the day of vengeance of our God. To comfort all who mourn, and provide for those who grieve in Zion— to bestow on them a crown of beauty instead of ashes, the oil of joy instead of mourning, and a garment of praise instead of a spirit of despair." (Isaiah 61:1)*

Life after Delivery

I once read an interesting story…

"In a mother's womb were two babies. One asked the other: "Do you believe in life after delivery?" The other replied, "Why, of course. There has to be something after delivery. Maybe we are here to prepare ourselves for what we will be later."

"Nonsense," said the first. "There is no life after delivery. What kind of life would that be?"

The second said, "I don't know, but maybe it will be lighter than here. Maybe we will walk with our legs and eat from our mouths. Maybe we will have other senses that we can't understand now."

The first replied, "That is absurd. Walking is impossible. And eating with our mouths? Ridiculous! The umbilical cord supplies nutrition and everything we need, but the umbilical cord is so short therefore life after delivery is to be logically excluded."

The second insisted, "Well I think there is something, and maybe it's different than it is here. Maybe we won't need this physical cord anymore."

The first replied, "Nonsense. And moreover, if there is life, then why has no one ever come back from there? Delivery is the end of life, and in the after-delivery, there is nothing but darkness and silence and oblivion. It takes us nowhere."

"Well, I don't know," said the second, "but certainly we will meet Mother and she will take care of us."

The first replied "Mother? You believe in Mother? That's laughable. If Mother exists then where is she now?"

The second said, "She is all around us. We are surrounded by her. We are of her. It is in her that we live. Without her, this world would not and could not exist."

The first said: "Well I don't see her, so it is only logical that she doesn't exist."

To which the second replied, "Sometimes when you're in silence, and you focus, and you really listen, you can perceive her presence, and you can hear her loving voice, calling down from above."

While experiencing unbearable grief, shameful and condemning guilt, and debilitating depression and anxiety was God preparing me for what I would later be? I often imagined what my life would be like after delivery. I was optimistic that the worse parts of my life would be over and that after delivery there was nothing but joyful noise and a life of more than enough ahead of me. I was confident that I would be able to walk upright no longer with my head held low because I believed that God is omnipotent and omnipresent therefore I would have all the strength that I need, knowing that He would never leave me or forsake me. I believed that it is in Him that I live, move and have by being; therefore, I will always be safe and protected. I knew that when things would become hectic in my life, I could silence myself and focus on Him and in His very presence I would find comfort, and His tranquil voice would direct me into all wisdom, knowledge, and understanding.

My Misery Ended in Missouri

Working for my employer had many perks and paid training were one of them. During one of our monthly all staff meetings we were informed that our agency was provided with a grant that would allow for two prevention specialists the opportunity to become trained trainers of a Mental Health First Aid Program in Missouri. It was explained that Mental Health First Aid is an eight-hour course that teaches you how to help someone who is developing a mental health problem or experiencing a mental health crisis. The training helps you identify, understand and respond to signs of addictions and mental illnesses. You learn; risk factors and warning signs of mental health problems and information on depression, anxiety, trauma, psychosis, and addiction disorders.

Upon hearing the news, I was elated. At the time I was currently going back to school to receive my Bachelor's degree in Mental Health Counseling and this training was a perfect fit. Not to mention the mental health crisis's that I experienced over the last few years because of that, I wanted to use my skills to help others. I believed that I was, in fact, the perfect candidate for the training. After expressing my desire to be one of the two trained, in only a short time later I was on my way to Kansas City, Missouri.

On 8/24/14, I landed in Kansas City, and I was excited yet nervous to begin my five-day training. Day one of the training was great; especially to see so many people from across the U.S come together on one accord, eager to learn the skills needed to help someone who's experiencing a mental health crisis. There were Psychologists from Virginia, Professionals from Maryland, but the one who stood out most was an African American woman who came from Texas. She strolled into the training room late as she used a walker to assist her. Since she was tardy, she missed out on our icebreaker introductions. Once she sat down the facilitators allowed her to introduce herself to the group. She began by apologizing for her tardiness and explained that she was recovering from a near-fatal car accident that she was involved in just a few months prior. She went on to say that she was an executive director at a nonprofit in Arlington Texas; where their philosophy was "Impacting our community from the Inside-Out" I guess it was her very evident strength and determination that made her stand out from the rest.

After learning and having to retain so much information in just four days 8/29/15, day five of the training was now upon us. It was the pivotal moment when each trainee had to successfully present a section of the material to receive their certification as a Mental Health First Aid Trainer. The topic I was given to present on was trauma. With a slight smile on my face, I laughingly shook my head and thought to myself "Lord, is this what you were preparing me for?" With all of the trauma that I have experienced in my life, and more so within the last few years it seemed only natural for me to be able to train someone on what a traumatic event is. The effects that a traumatic event can have on a person and provide them with the information to help others through a traumatic event. Although I felt that trauma was an ideal topic for me to present on I was on the other hand very nervous because I was afraid that I was too connected to the material, which could potentially lead me to be more transparent about my experiences than what I felt they would accept. In my mind I was battling with what I was taught about self-disclosure while presenting vs. what I believe about transparency during presentations. While quieting myself to quickly rehearse the material I prepared I heard that same tranquil voice I often hear when I'm in need of wisdom and direction whisper "remain true to you." As my name was called next to present, I felt a peace and calmness come over me. I obeyed the voice, and I remained faithful to me. Without being specific, I shared how I experienced some traumatic times in my life, how I connected with the material and how important it is to help someone through their traumatic event. As I sat and looked out in the audience I can tell that the participants were receptive as their heads nodded up and down in agreement, their eyes were fixated on my every move and gesture and as they applauded at the close of my presentation.

As I was taking my seat, the woman from Texas began to share her experience of being in a near fatal car accident. With teary eyes, she stated how she often prays for the woman who hit her and wonders if the woman thinks about her and the pain that she caused. Listening to her questions and the emotion in which she asked I couldn't help but to become very emotional myself.

It was as if she was directing those concerns to me and I somehow felt responsible for answering them for her. I felt like she was my victim and I was her offender. I became anxious, similar to when a teacher, without notice, calls on you in front of the class to give an answer, and you're caught off guard. My stomach was in knots, and there was a huge lump in my throat, my heart began to race increasingly, and my hands instantly became sweaty. As I took a few slow deep breaths in and out to regulate my breathing, and as I wiped my eyes from the tears that immediately began to fall, before I could open my mouth to reply our trainer made the announcement that it was time to take a break. Still feeling responsible for answering her question I remained in my seat momentarily, considering, what my next step would be. While looking at her from across the room, I was compelled to share with her my traumatic event in brief detail. Seemingly moving in slow motion, I quickly gathered the courage to approach her. As I looked her in the eyes, I told her how the words she shared pierced my soul. I began to share details about a fatal car accident that I was responsible for that claimed the life of another. I expressed how I often think about the woman I hit and the intense feelings of depression, guilt and anxiety often overwhelming me so much so that I couldn't seem to forgive myself.

After quietly, passionately and Non-judgmentally listening to me her silence was broken as she softly but yet fervently said to me "On behalf of Deborah, I forgive you." Immediately my body went limp; we cried together, and I could hear the sounds of chains hitting the floor.   Those seven words were the keys that I used to unchain my shackles and make me free. Whoever said "forgiveness isn't about the other person, it's a gift you give yourself" Lied! Her forgiveness was my gift. Forgiveness is a gift that keeps on giving. Some would say it's Karma, but I believe the word of God in (Matthew 6:14) is true *"If you forgive those who sin against you, your heavenly Father will forgive you."* As traumatic as the offenses of my son's molestation and my rape were for me to forgive, I did, I told our offenders that I forgave them. Hopefully with my gift of forgiveness they were able to free themselves of guilt and shame.

My years of the raging war in my mind were finally over. My day of independence had finally come. That's when I realized "He turned it and gave me beauty for ashes!"

After the accident, years before going to Missouri, God voiced to me that part of my mission was "to proclaim freedom for the captive, release from darkness the prisoners and to comfort all who mourn." He instructed me to do this by facilitating restorative conferences between victims and offenders. In criminal justice, restorative conferences allow victims, offenders and their respective family members and friends the chance to come together to explore how everyone has been affected by an offense and, when possible, to decide how to repair the harm and meet their needs.

Knowing that this is what God intended for me to do, I felt a bit unenthusiastic at times. I often thought about how unfair it would be for me to be able to facilitate such powerful healing between a victim and an offender and I not personally understand how it feels to benefit from that level of healing.

As I look back on that day with tears in my eyes. I can't help but pause and take a moment to thank God! I thank Him because He's so mindful of me, I thank Him because He knows my beginning from my end, I thank Him because He knows my heart and what I stand in need of, I Thank Him because He's strategic and purposeful. I thank Him for my birthing and delivery process. I thank Him because He has truly given me a garment of praise instead of a spirit of despair.

As that fifth day of training came to a close, I received a letter from Tavian, and it read:

My dear sister,

"I wanted to drop you a line that will keep you encouraged. First of all, thank you for sharing your story with me. Secondly, always remember God is not just good; HE IS GREAT! We did not just meet by accident it was ALL in His plan for our lives.

Court, trust yourself, and believe in you! God has great plans for your life. Know that. My organization is Seasons of Change-I change seasons! Your season has changed!

However here are some specific things God wants you to do in this season:

- *Trust Him*
- *Write Your Book*
- *Write your plan for your Ministry*
- *LOVE YOU!*
- *Give yourself to Prayer & Fasting*
- *BE HAPPY-SMILE-KEEP IT MOVING*

As I look at you now: 11:40 am 8/29/14 I see the wind at your back. There is such a glow in your spirit. God has touched your spirit and soul. Now I am not saying there will not be hard days because there will be, that is the enemy's job, and he does it well. However, you are no longer the person you were! God has touched the core of your very being. My dear sister walk in your liberty, walk in freedom and walk in the purpose God has given you!

Love Tavian!"

She was right! My season had changed and from that day forth I began to walk in freedom and purpose. A few months later I fulfilled my dream and became a Grief Recovery Specialist; I now comfort individuals who are grieving. I help them to understand that grief is the normal and natural reaction to a personal loss of any kind that extends beyond death. It's experienced by all no matter if you're the offender of a crime, victim or loved one. As every relationship is unique, so are the feelings and thoughts each person will have concerning the relationship that has been altered by a loss. I provide people with helpful and healthy information and action steps that will support them to move beyond the pain caused by loss. I help them to examine their beliefs about coping with loss; to look at what losses have affected their life; and to take new actions which will lead them to the completion of the pain attached to one of those losses to live a more healthy, happy and productive life.

My ministry was birthed from a broken heart and a humble spirit. Much like any natural birthing process, there's hurt and pain. There were some things I had to endure and push my way through. However when I was delivered, the cord of bondage was cut, and I was no longer bound on the inside but free, just like a baby, I cried out loud! When I was delivered I forget all about the pain, my past was now behind me, and I realized that I had to experience some pain and be removed from my comfort zone to be free and to free others. Once I was broken, humbled and healed by the King of kings my tears were not tears of sorrow or pain but they were tears of someone who was unmasked before God, not ashamed to cry out to Him in worship and adoration because I understood that only the Father could make me whole. I didn't care about what people may think or what crowd was around. Just like the woman with the issue of blood, I understood that I needed to touch Him and wasn't ashamed to go out into the crowd to get my healing. Similar to her I tried physicians, friends, and self -medicating for years but no one or nothing was able to heal me.

I guess Tye Tribett was truthful when he expressed; "The worse thing in my whole life became the most beautiful thing."

9

<u>MY FOUNDATION</u>

In 2015, committed to my purpose I established Broken Branches Inc. with a mission to comfort those who mourn, restore healthy relationships, and increase mental illness awareness in our communities with the hope that individuals live a more healthy, abundant and productive life.

Broken Branches

For months I found myself fascinated by a tree outside of my office window. This tree raised two and a half stories high and was full of branches covered with green leaves. It was a refreshing site to see and in some ways, it rejuvenated me by simply watching it. What captivated me the most about this tree was how a single broken branch that fell from the top of the tree managed to fasten itself to another branch below it securely, as the high winds blew, the tree remained firm, strong and unmoved. The branches attached to the tree quivered, but they never became detached.

Day after day for at least two months as I began to observe and study this tree it was astonishing to me that as the winds blew the broken branch continued to grip itself to the attached branch as if it were holding on for dear life. I became so engrossed by this broken branch that there were times I would just pause my duties for the moment and sit and watch. Times when I had a free moment, I would sit and watch. Times when I became stressed, I would just sit and watch. Coming back to work on a Monday morning after a weekend off to see this branch was like watching your favorite drama on television each week, and when it goes off, you're left in suspense as you begin to speculate what will happen next week.

As fixated as I had become with this branch it was now 4:00 pm and my shift had just ended. The weekend of Friday, the 13th 2006 was here and after a much stressful week I was preparing for some time of rest. While listening to the radio in the car on my way home, I heard the news of a storm warning. It called for one to three inches of snow, with possible accumulations of up to six inches. The notice also made specific mention of possible tree damage and power outages. Living in Buffalo, NY it was not uncommon for us to experience all four season in a week. My thought was perhaps the meteorologists were incorrect about the storm and at the most we will receive just a few inches of snow, what's the problem?

But to my surprise, they were accurate this time. The drastic change of weather began with small hail and ice pellets followed by rain and snow mix, which later turned into the rain changing over entirely to snow with the temperature dropping from 41 degrees F to 33.8 degrees F in less than two hours. To us locals, it was the beginning of what would become known as the shock called "The October Storm." To others, it was described as astounding, unbelievable and incredible. According to the National Weather Service, it was reported as "the worst October lake effect snow storm in 137 years of records" being kept. The NOAA called the weather event "unprecedented." The Toronto Star referenced this storm as "one of the most devastating snow storms in the US history." 300,000 homes and businesses were without power. Many people including myself had to stay with family or friends due to lack of food and electricity outages in their homes. Some were stranded in airports and couldn't return home. There were piles of snow onto trees which were still in full leaf, which lead to significant damage to trees on a scale usually associated with hurricanes. 90 percent of the city's trees were estimated to be damaged; including many in the city's cherished parks and parkways. Cleanup efforts were impeded in the first days after the storm by the tangle of fallen trees, fallen branches and downed power lines. Effects of this storm were responsible for over ten fatalities two of which were from automobile accidents and one from a falling branch.

After about four days from the storms inception, the driving band was lifted, and minimum cleanup efforts were made and I along with many others were allowed to report back to work. While sitting at my desk, I began to ponder on the series of events that had transpired over the past few days. Much like the passing of a loved one an event of this magnitude causes you to put your life into proper perspective. As I was doing just that I found myself at my desk gazing out of the same window that I had looked out of so many times before. When I did, I noticed the "broken branch" was still fastened to the attached limb. In a state of shock and bewilderment as tears immediately began to fill my eyes I remember calling "JESUS!" After hearing the news reports and witnessing how this storm wreaked havoc upon the city and mainly its trees I couldn't believe that this broken branch was still holding on.

It was at that very moment that this broken branch became much more to me than just a detached limb on a tree, it became a personal message that I had to decode. For me, this limb seemed to put into perspective that there is in fact "Life after Death." I started to quiet myself and inquire of the Lord the message behind this broken branch. So with pen and paper in hand, I began to write down what I heard the Lord say, *(2 Tim 2:11-12) "For if we be dead with Him, we shall also live with Him, If we suffer with him we shall also reign with Him."* I understood the broken branch represents those that are broken and for whatever reasons they have went astray and allowed life's storms, test, and trials to separate them from God. The branches that are still attached to the tree are those individuals who are in a relationship with God, still connected to Him. The broken branch and the branch supporting it both exemplify the body of Christ and the relationship that we should have with one another. In Ephesians, it explains that we are the body of Christ and describes how we are jointly fit together supplying what the other needs. The positioning of the broken branch before it fell is also something to take note of. This branch fell from the top of the tree and was once in a higher position than the branch it safely secured itself to during its fall. I began to think about how people we consider to be of higher status, such as the leaders of our churches, states, countries, organizations, and families all around the world can and will what we commonly refer to as "Fall from grace." They will require the support and love of those under and around them to catch them before they hit the ground, those who are willing to attach themselves to someone whose broken to support them in a non-judgmental way, with loving kindness, and a spirit of meekness.

Close your eyes and take a moment to think about a time or circumstance in your life where you were so overwhelmed that you felt like whatever you were going through was too much for you to bear alone. Perhaps you thought about throwing in the towel and giving up on the situation, or maybe you even decided that you had enough with life and were contemplating suicide. This situation could be a sickness, any form of abuse, miscarriage, divorce, loss of a loved one or even a job loss. Hold on to that memory and briefly reflect on the emotions that gripped you and the state of mind you were in because of it. Now imagine for a moment that you are standing on the ledge of a high standing building contemplating jumping off because of this unbearable and painful situation. Below you are friends and loved ones trying to talk you off the ledge. Their saying things like we love you, it's not your fault, don't give up, we understand and we're here to help. Even though they are empathetically offering you words of comfort and wisdom, you still find no solace within. Chock-full of hurt and anger you make a split second decision and determine within yourself that no one understands the weight of your burden ultimately deciding to jump. As you speedily plummet your way down to what will eventually be your demise with no chance of reversing what you had just done you suddenly stop short of the ground and as you open your eyes you realize that the persons below you who were consoling you have reached out to catch you, and you are still alive! Not only are you alive but now all of your weight and the weight of the burdens you once carried alone are being supported by others.

Just like the broken branch outside of my window after its fall it was because of the support that the branch still attached to the tree offered that the broken branch didn't fall to the ground. The supportive branch had to remain strong while carrying the burden of the broken branch because if it were to break and fall, it would force the broken branch attached to it to collapse as well. I've said and have heard others say, "I have to remain strong because _____ is counting on me." Carrying the weight of someone or something else can often bring about added stress and pain to the one who is supporting it. Have you ever been in a situation where you had to offer support to someone else while at the same time trying to find a solution and obtain support for your needs? Particularly during these financially trying times, many are facing. Most people are without pay, underpaid or have to seek financial aid from family and friends. It can be sometimes daunting to receive a call from someone asking to borrow money to pay their bills and forced to make a decision knowing that you too stand in need of help. However you choose to give it to them anyway while looking to God for support, having the faith to believe that He will supply your needs. It was important for the branch to remain attached to the tree because alone it's not capable of offering that type of support. It needed something stronger than itself to support it as it continued to carry the weight of something else. In (Mat 11:28) it reads: "Come unto me all [ye] that labor and are heavy laden and I will give you rest." It's important for us to remain connected to our strength and power source which is in God when trying to carry any heavy burdens or weights that belong to ourselves or others which can cause us to become weary. *(Galatians 6:1-2) shows us how we are supposed to support one another. "Brethren, if a man be overtaken in a fault, ye which are spiritual, restore such as one in the spirit of meekness, considering thyself, lest thou also be tempted. Bear ye one another's burdens, and so fulfill the law of Christ."*

Relationships and connections are vital to our well-being. We cannot exist on our own. It's impossible to give yourself a label without connecting yourself to someone or something else. I can't say that I'm a mother, daughter, sister, friend or employee without connecting myself to my parents, son, brother, friends or employer. In Genesis, God said it's not good for man to be alone so from Adam He created Eve and from the dust He created Adam. These relationships should be healthy and interdependent. Interdependence is a relationship in which each member is mutually dependent on the other. These relationships help us to know who we are and promote growth. Research shows that all of us need other people to be well and thrive. We feel better by just being around other people, and close relationships tend to make us happy. Think about a time when you were lonely or sad and how just the simple connection of a loved one provided you some much-needed comfort and support. Some characteristics of close relationships are:

- *Caring*
- *Security*
- *Support*
- *Mutual understanding*
- *Validation of self-worth*
- *The ability to love and be loved*
- *A source of direct help in times of trouble*

Belonging to a particular group or a community gives us a sense of identity. It helps us understand who we are and causes us to feel a part of something larger than ourselves. Researchers also find that people with strong social connections have less stress-related health problems, lower risk of mental illness, and faster recovery from trauma or illness.

As I look over my life, I realize that the same horrific conditions that I've faced were not exclusive to me but in fact, others have encountered these same experiences, but unfortunately, they did not yield the same outcome. Some have committed suicide, led lives of promiscuity, been institutionalized or have not yet begun to turn their mess into a message and live a life of purpose. Many people say that they stand in awe because as I tell my story what they hear and what they see doesn't match. They say, "You don't look like what you've been through" and I smile in agreement. They can't comprehend how I've managed to survive and get through these trying times without harming myself, but they didn't realize that it wasn't due to a lack of trying. Some have sought to give the credit to me and even though I'll say yes, I had to actively play a part in my recovery. However, I will admit, I attribute most of it to the fact that in my times of brokenness and despair it was the faithfulness of my loved ones that attached themselves to me with a spirit of meekness as they remained connected to the True and Living Vine. So that when I did fall I didn't fall to the ground and die like many others, but instead they reached out to catch me and helped me carry and ultimately release the weight of some of my heaviest burdens.

I then asked God, "but how can the broken branch reattach itself to the tree and begin to bear fruit again?" Then the Lord said, "it must die and be replanted in good soil so that this time it's as strong as the tree and give birth to other branches that will bear fruit." Confused, I said, "but, God you are the tree. How can we replant and become you?" He replied: "It's not that the new tree is God, but that you were made in my image."

Much like the broken branch in this story, I would have faced a spiritual and physical death had it not been for the continual love and support of these individuals talking me off the ledge and catching me when I fell/fall. God gives us all broken branches to minister to. He understands that the power and strength that He has placed inside of us is not to be selfishly used for ourselves but to uplift those in their time of need. I thank Him for thoughtfully and strategically placing these very special people in my life. Knowing that they were equipped and strong enough to supply just what I stood in need of during my times of despair. To my mother **Charlotte**, thank you for showing me how to be a strong, independent and a respectful young lady. You've shown me the significance of adorning myself with self-respect and integrity. You've defined for me the meaning of perseverance by not allowing your disability or imperfect health to cripple you instead you continue to fight and demonstrate daily what resiliency means. You continue to selfishly support your family often times putting the needs of others before your own. I continue to draw strength from the strength that you exude from within. Your love for me goes without saying but is demonstrated in all that you do for me. I LOVE YOU! My son **Davon**, you saved my life! You are my joy and my heartbeat. You see the behind closed doors me and still love me the same. You push and motivate me to be a better me! You continue to teach me every day the importance of living my BEST life and the limitless possibilities it has to offer and "That's what's up!" I'm honored and humbled that God gave me you. I LOVE YOU! My big sister **Stephanie**, I didn't grow up with a sister but when you and I met it was as if you've been there all along. You're an awesome sister, and you serve as a great demonstration of what a Woman of God is. You made me become comfortable saying those three small yet impactful words; "I love you." You've taught me to pray "Lord, show me how to love you more so that in return I can love your people." Thank you for laughing with me, crying with me, praying for me, protecting me, and pushing me. Thank you for being brutally honest with me, being someone I can trust and confide in. Thank you for keeping me grounded and helping me to walk in fairness and love.

You've shown me that miracles still do happen and that with hard work, dedication and God nothing is impossible!! To my Pastor**, Darrell Fairer**, Thank you for watching over me spiritually and naturally, opening your home to me and talking me off of the ledge so many times. You've taught and shown me what real ministry is all about, never giving me the option to give up when things got rough but instead you offered me words that I live by today "When will we be healed enough to heal someone else." Under your leadership, I've learned the importance of humbly covering, protecting and serving leaders at ALL times. Thank you for teaching me how to be an I.M.P.A.C.T! To my Best Friend, First Lady **Sherea Fairer,** It's a privilege and an honor to serve you but at some point, I looked to my side and noticed that you were there to serve me. You have and continue to teach me so much about what it means to be a humble servant and dedicated Woman of God. Your pure love for God and His people is remarkable. With you, I can take my mask off and exhale. We've laughed and cried together proving that you love me flaws and all, the good, bad and the ugly. My "Golden Girl" the friend that I'll grow old and gray with. Thank you for being a friend. You saw and continue to see things in me that I don't see myself. Thank you for encouraging me and pushing me towards Greater! To My **Wonder Woman Sisters**, the transparency, openness, support and unconditional love that I experienced 11/14 has forever changed my life. My **PREVENTIONFOCUS** family THANK YOU for believing in me and for your support. To my Spiritual parents **Frank Scott Sr. and Sheila Scott** you guys are HEAVEN SENT!! Thank you for adopting me and loving me as one of your own. When I'm with you guys it feels like "home!" Pastor **Denise Millben**, THANK YOU for love without judgement and condemnation! My cousin's **Brittany and Brianna**, two amazing Women of God, THANK YOU! This book wouldn't be complete without your inspiring words. **Dawn Flakes**, Your words are life to me, THANK YOU for standing in the gap for me, standing up for me, and standing with me through the highs and the lows. **Anissa**, my "mini me", my little sister, my big daughter, my mentee, my road dog, my heart! It simply amazes me how you believe and look up to me, and I don't take it for granted. I vow to always be your imperfectly imperfect role model. You're my constant reminder that I'm charged to mentor! My sister **Felicia** and cousin **Angel**, there were so many times that the thought of you two, your perseverance and very evident strength made me believe that I can do it too! You never gave up, and you continued to push yourselves beyond any barriers. I LOVE YOU! **Donna Williams** "Mom" from the moment I laid eyes on you I said "I want to be like her when I grow up." You came into my life at the perfect time. Your presence, love, attention, lessons are revitalizing me and give me hope for a fresh start. You remind me of the beautiful princess that I am and you assure me that you love and support me flaws and all. Thank you for not just "loving me but liking me!" **Tavian** – with your help 8/29 marks my independence day –the day when my misery ended in Missouri. I never thought that self-forgiveness was possible for me until you said the life changing words "on behalf of Deborah I forgive you." Thank you for saying the phrase, which unlocked the chains to make me free. Special thanks to **Cheryl Baker** (R.I.P) meeting you has forever changed my life, with a smile, you were the first to ask "Why don't you know who you are?" Thank you for opening my mind and eyes to discover the "me" I didn't see. Thank you for seeing past my mask. **Karyn Washington**, I vow to keep your name and mission alive. I vow to do my all to raise the importance of mental illnesses awareness for brown girls and women of all colors and shades in our communities. I vow to help restore joy to all those who have lost it, so that they'll know that suicide isn't the only way to escape their pain, but instead showing them that they can lean on others for their life, health, and strength.

10

EMBRACELET

In My Lane

Ready for a change, in spite of the 50 percent chance of rain I decided one day to begin walking again, but I didn't want to do it alone. I guess I thought the support and company would've made the 1.76-mile walk which seemed more like 1,000 miles to a novice walker like me around Delaware Park easier to accomplish. Not to mention the thought of embarking on a new journey alone wasn't something I was comfortable with just yet. Feeling afraid, yet determined I convinced myself that I could do it alone.

Once I arrived at the park, I sat in my car for a few minutes scoping out the walkers some walking in pairs and others alone. As I got out of my car, I began my seemingly 1,000-mile journey around the park. When I took the first step, I remembered the quote by Lao Tzu- "The journey of a thousand mile begins with a simple step." So while looking up at the dark clouds, breathing in a deep breath and slowly exhaling I proceeded to take another step after step towards my journey.

There's a lot you discover about yourself when you walk alone. In the short distance between my car and the path, I began studying the other walkers. What they were wearing, how they were walking, who they were walking with, what they were walking with, the speed in which they were walking, if they were quiet or talking when walking, and if the walkers were younger or older than me. All of these things I used to measure myself as a walker. That's when I learned the harsh reality that I compare myself to others.

It's sometimes said that one indication of someone who has high self-esteem is that they walk with their head held high. With each step I took, I noticed that my mind was focused, my back was straight, and my head was high. Once I became more focused on the goal before me, I gained momentum and then started noticing that I was surpassing those walkers who were once ahead of me. In the beginning, when I realized that I was just steps away from approaching and passing them I began to slow down my pace because I felt it was somehow wrong to exceed them.

Naturally, when walking a path with others, you will find both leaders and followers. Some will lead you as they walk and pave the way for you and others you will lead as they walk behind you. Often the one thing that separates us from exceeding the person walking before us is a single step. Don't be afraid to take the next step because those that you are leading are expecting you to keep it moving. Perhaps it was their lack of drive or maybe they became relaxed and began to operate in cruise control which allowed them to slow their pace. Whatever the case that's not your problem. In those quick moments, I recalled Marianne Willaimson, who said "You're playing small does not serve the world. There is nothing enlightened about shrinking so that other people won't feel insecure around you…. As we let our own light shine, we unconsciously give other people permission to do the same."

I started to ponder on how I was dimming my own light by playing small, attempting to mirror the role models and mentors that I admired for so long. Those teachers, mentors, friends, public persona's, supervisors, etc. that paved the way for me, whose greatness I wanted so much to emulate. I recalled the different times I sought their advice and direction when I was yet searching for "the way." In some way, I was hoping that they could be the light to my path. Optimistic that they could "fix my life" when I was still broken on the inside. Confident that if I could just attach myself to one of their names, names that I perceived to be higher and more important than my own that I too can be someone just as big as they are. After all, I've often heard it said: "your network determines your net worth."

Searching and searching for the one perfect person that I could emulate, I couldn't seem to find the one that was just right. It was like the story of the three little bears: Either they were too dictatorial and condescending, not transparent enough, they didn't share my personal beliefs and standards or they just didn't seem to see my bigger picture.

A few months prior, while on my quest for the ideal mentor who would lead me and guide me into the greatness that I knew was on the inside of me. I discovered and seized the opportunity to attend the "Wonder Woman Weekend" facilitated by "My mentor (in my head), Iyanla Vanzant." After an incredible weekend of self-reflection, meditation, sisterhood, and healing I had reached the conclusion of the weekend. While sitting in a front row seat, directly facing Iylanla I was in awe of her, and after following her for so many years, way back to her "Starting Over" days I felt for so long that she was my "just right", but yet while sitting in front of her this day I couldn't help but feel like she wasn't the one and that my pursuit of the one was still on. Sitting in a front row seat, directly facing Iylanla I was in awe of her. After following her for so many years, way back to her "Starting Over" days, I felt for so long that she was my "just right." Seated in front of her this day, I couldn't help but to question if she was the one, or if my pursuit of the one was still on. As I sat there, God told me "spell mentor" as a thirty- three-year-old woman, I laughed to myself, not answering, thinking about how trivial and elementary of a question it was. Being persistent, He asked me as only a teacher could "spell mentor." Like a child who hears their parent repeat a question I knew this wasn't a rhetorical question and that it would be in my best interest to answer the question. So I did, saying to myself slowly one letter at a time m...e...n...t...o...r. "That was easy, See, God I know how to spell", I said. Then He said, "Spell it again." Smiling, but yet confused I started to spell it again. Slowly, one letter at a time "m...e...n" and once I got to "t", His point was becoming clear to me. I restarted, this time, envisioning the letters as I was saying them. However, this time, I wasn't slow, getting the revelation I began to spell it with speed "m.e.n.T.o.r" it was as if the once lower case "t" in the word immediately began to rise and became "T" which represented the cross. Once I received the revelation that's when God asked me "who are you going to follow men or Christ (T)?"

It was at that moment, I realized what I was searching for in others to do I already had the power within myself to perform. A mirror is used to reflect a clear image, but my life's circumstances began to cloud the once clear image I had of myself. The only way for me to regain a clear image of myself was to remember to see myself the way God created me. Then I recalled *(Genesis 1:27)* "*So God created man in his own image, in the image of God, created He him; male and female created He them.*" Suddenly, Jimmy Cliff's song had a brand new meaning. ***"I can see clearly now the rain is gone/ I can see all obstacles in my way/ Gone are the dark clouds that had me blind/ Oh, yes I can make it now the pain is gone/All of the bad feelings have disappeared/Here is that rainbow I've been praying for/ It's gonna be a bright (bright) sunshiny day"***

I had to understand that it wasn't in them to direct my path and order my steps. Instead knowing that according *to (Psalm 37:23) "The steps of a good man are ordered by the Lord: and He delights in his way."* Then *(Psalms 119:105)* **reminds** me *"Your word is a lamp to guide my feet and a light for my path."*

I discovered that not everyone's walk during their life's journey will look the same. What works for one doesn't work for all. For me to be the best I can be it requires me simply be me. After all "Variety is the spice of life." Right? It was liberating when I was finally able to grasp that I don't have to compare myself to anyone else. That if the path becomes too crowded I can create my own lane. Now I live by the motto "In my lane loving my life."

A Tough Pill to Swallow

One morning my son said that he didn't want to attend school saying that he didn't feel well. Instead, he wanted to lie around at home until his pains went away. As his mother, I knew my child enough to say to him "you'll be OK and you're going to school." Of course, he persisted that he didn't feel well and should stay home. I offered him medicine by way of what I perceived to be a small pill. Confident that if he took the medicine, the pain would go away. However, he whimpered and complained that the pill was too big to swallow. Immediately I became furious and irate because at that moment I felt he was demonstrating weakness as a young man. I told him that I would not allow him to dismiss or neglect his responsibilities because of a little pain. Nor will he be allowed to lay down when he refuses to take part in his recovery (swallow the pill). I proceeded to tell him that if he didn't take the medicine to get better, he better not call me later for help (tough love). My son did not take the medicine because he perceived it to be a big/tough pill to swallow and went to school in spite of his pain.

What's the lesson, "Dr. Courtney?" How many of us are asking God for help in taking the pain away but are too afraid to take His prescribed medication because it's a big/tough pill to swallow? We would rather lay comfortable in our pain and expect Him to baby us instead of choosing to participate in our own recovery. As our father who loves us more than we can comprehend. I'm certain that He gets frustrated with us when we ask for but don't receive His way of help. We are asking God to remove us from an unhealthy relationship but won't swallow the pill. We are asking Him to heal us but won't swallow the pill. We are asking Him to increase our finances but won't swallow the pill. We are asking him to restore what's broken but won't swallow the pill.

Today, I dare you to take self-inventory. What pain(s) do you have that persists in your life that only remains because you're too afraid to swallow the pill? Unfortunately, the responsibilities and purpose you have won't go away because of the pain, but you have a choice, you can do your work in pain or healed. The choice is yours.

Extractions

For me to experience healing, wholeness and a life without pain I had to give up something that I carried around for years, I was too afraid to remove it because I was terrified of the process and the temporary pain the extraction would cause me. So for years I walked around in pain and bleeding from holes within, while only receiving temporary relief from self-medicating. Until one day while trying to enjoy life, the pain suddenly became too unbearable, and I was forced to make a life-altering decision.

I decided that although I was still afraid and unsure of the process. I wanted and deserved to be healed and whole, so I chose to let go of that thing that I thought I needed but caused me great pain. Although it was physically and visually obvious to me that what I once had I'm now without, it was worth it because now I can say that I'm painless, no longer bleeding and healed. I realized that wholeness doesn't mean the lack of extractions from your life. It means that in spite of those subtractions, I have everything that I need to be complete.

Even though this specific removal was a decayed tooth, the principle remains the same and can be applied to other areas in my life. There was a time that I believed in error that I needed to hold on to guilt, shame, and unforgiveness of self but the pain of holding on to those feelings became too intense and unbearable that living an abundant life seemed impossible. I made a life changing decision to let go of those errors in my mind so that I can embrace deliverance, healing, and wholeness in my life. While I was healing my emotional wounds; it was important for me not to concentrate or feed upon the experience, as that would've only reinforced the reasons why I was hurt, guilty, shameful or angry. Think about it, if you had two flowers and you watered and gave sunlight to one and starved the other which one would remain alive? The one you fed of course.

I understood that it was my reaction to what was done to me or what I did that held me in bondage and torture. The unforgiveness, guilt, and anger kept me chained. I had to accept the truth which was, I wasn't responsible for what was done to me, and I had to forgive myself for the things that I was responsible for. I had to take accountability for how I chose to react to those things I did and those things that were done to me. When I struck the woman with my car, it wasn't the accident that caused the bondage but instead it was how I internalized the accident that caused those feelings to remain and affect me well after the incident.

Embracing the truth and letting go of the lies that I told myself was a process for me and continues to be a practice that I carry out on a daily basis. Just as I accept brand new mercies and grace for myself in the mornings daily, I also make a conscious effort to embrace something positive and let go of something negative. What lies are you telling yourself that you should let go of? What truths do you need to embrace?

Here's something more to consider. If an officiant of a wedding can have faith in a state to declare; "By the power vested in me by the state of _____I now pronounce you_____." And it is so, then why as believers of

Christ are we not as faithful and bold to pronounce some things over our lives and the lives of others?

I "Dr. Courtney Hawkins", a Minister and follower of Christ, by the power vested in me by the Holy Spirit, now pronounce you Free, Healed, Blessed, and Whole, in EVERY ASPECT OF YOUR LIFE....IN JESUS NAME, so be it.

EMBRACE THAT!

Like what you read? Go to Amazon and add a book review.
To contact or book "Dr. Courtney"
Visit:
drcourtneyspeaks@gmail.com
Like us on Facebook www.AuthorCourtneyHawkins

<u>NOTES</u>